Introduction to Programming with Greenfoot

**Companion Website**
Additional material and resources for this book can be found at
**http://www.greenfoot.org/book/**

**For students:**
- The Greenfoot software
- The scenarios discussed in this book
- The Greenfoot Gallery—a scenario showcase
- Tutorial videos
- A discussion forum
- Technical support

**For teachers:**
- A teacher discussion forum
- Additional exercises related to the book
- The "Green Room" containing worksheets and other teaching
  resources

# Introduction to Programming with Greenfoot

## Object-Oriented Programming in Java™ with Games and Simulations

Michael Kölling

**Prentice Hall**

Upper Saddle River · Boston · Columbus · San Francisco · New York
Indianapolis · London · Toronto · Sydney · Singapore · Tokyo · Montreal · Dubai
Madrid · Hong Kong · Mexico City · Munich · Paris · Amsterdam · Cape Town

**Vice President and Editorial Director, ECS:** *Marcia J. Horton*
**Editor in Chief, CS:** *Michael Hirsch*
**Executive Editor:** *Tracy Dunkelberger*
**Assistant Editor:** *Melinda Haggerty*
**Editorial Assistant:** *Allison Michael*
**Director of Team-Based Project Management:** *Vince O'Brien*
**Senior Managing Editor:** *Scott Disanno*
**Production Liaison:** *Irwin Zucker*
**Production Editor:** *Shiny Rajesh, Integra*
**Senior Operations Specialist:** *Alan Fischer*
**Operation Specialist:** *Lisa McDowell*
**Marketing Manager:** *Erin Davis*
**Marketing Coordinator:** *Kathryn Ferranti*
**Art Director:** *Jayne Conte*
**Cover Designer:** *Bruce Kenselaar*
**Art Editor:** *Greg Dulles*
**Media Editor:** *Daniel Sandin*
**Composition/Full-Service Project Management:** *Integra*

**Library of Congress Cataloging-in-Publication Data on File**

10 9 8 7 6 5 4 3 2 1

**Prentice Hall**
is an imprint of

www.pearsonhighered.com

ISBN-13: 978-0-13-603753-8
ISBN-10:    0-13-603753-4

To Krümel and Cracker—may their imagination never fade.

—*mk*

Education is not the filling of a pail, but the lighting of a fire.

—*William Butler Yeats*

# Contents

# List of scenarios discussed in this book

**Leaves and wombats** (Chapter 1)

This is a simple example showing wombats moving around on screen, occasionally eating leaves. The scenario has no specific purpose other than illustrating some important object-oriented concepts and Greenfoot interactions.

**Asteroids 1** (Chapter 1)

This is a simple version of a classic arcade game. You fly a spaceship through space and try to avoid being hit by asteroids. At this stage, we only use the scenario to make some small changes and illustrate some basic concepts.

**Little Crab** (Chapter 2)

This is our first full development. Starting from almost nothing, we develop a simple game slowly, adding may things such as movement, keyboard control, sound, and many other elements of typical games.

**Piano** (Chapter 5)

An on-screen piano that you can really play.

**Newton's Lab** (Chapter 6)

*Newton's Lab* is a simulation of the motion of stars and planets in space. Gravity plays a central role here. We also make a variant of this that combines gravity with making music, ending up with musical output triggered by objects under gravitational movement.

**Asteroids 2** (Chapter 7)

We come back to the asteroids example from Chapter 2. This time, we investigate more fully how to implement it.

**Ants** (Chapter 9)

A simulation of ant colonies searching for food, communicating via drops of pheromones left on the ground.

**The following scenarios are presented in Chapter 10 and selected aspects of them briefly discussed. They are intended as inspiration for further projects.**

**Marbles**

A simulation of a marble board game. Marbles have to be cleared of the board within a limited number of moves. Contains simple physics.

### Lifts

A start of a lift simulation. Incomplete at this stage—can be used as a start of a project.

### Boids

A demo showing flocking behavior: A flock of birds flies across the screen, aiming to stick together while avoiding obstacles.

### Circles

Make patterns in different colors on the screen with moving circles.

### Explosion

A demo of a more sophisticated explosion effect.

### Breakout

This is the start of an implementation of the classic Breakout game. Very incomplete, but with an interesting visual effect.

### Platform jumper

A demo of a partial implementation of an ever-popular genre of games: platform jumpers.

### Wave

This scenario is a simple demonstration of a physical effect: the propagation of a wave on a string.

# Preface

Greenfoot is a programming environment that can be used by individuals, in schools or in introductory university courses to learn and teach the principles of programming. It is flexible enough to be suitable for teenagers as well as older students.

Greenfoot supports the Java Programming Language, so students learn standard object-oriented programming in Java. The environment is designed specifically to convey object-oriented concepts and principles in a clean, easily accessible manner.

The Greenfoot environment makes creation of graphics and interaction easy. Students can concentrate on modifying the application logic, and engage and experiment with objects. Developing simulations and interactive games becomes easy, and feedback is immediate.

The environment is designed to quickly engage students who may have no prior interest or experience in programming. Achieving simple animation results is quick, sophisticated, professional looking scenarios are possible.

## Accessing Supplementary Materials

The learning aids and supplementary materials that are noted in the book can be accessed through the Greenfoot Companion Web site or through the publisher's Web site:

**Companion Website:** http://www.greenfoot.org/book/
**Publisher's Website:** http://www.prenhall.com/kolling

## Supplementary Materials Available for Students

The following supplements are available for students:

- The Greenfoot software
- The scenarios discussed in this book
- The Greenfoot Gallery—a scenario showcase
- Tutorial videos
- A discussion forum
- Technical support

## Supplementary Materials Available for Instructors

The following supplements are available for instructors:

- A teacher discussion forum
- Additional exercises related to the book
- The "Green Room" containing worksheets and other teaching resources

For more details about Greenfoot and this book, please also see the Introduction following the Acknowledgments.

# Acknowledgments

This book is the result of more than five years of work by a group of people. First and foremost involved are the people who contributed to the development of the Greenfoot environment, which makes this entire educational approach possible. Poul Henriksen started the implementation of Greenfoot as his Masters project and built the first prototype. He also took on the development of this prototype into a production system. For the first year or so, we were a two-man project, and Poul's work led to the quality and robustness of the current system.

Bruce Quig and Davin McCall were the next developers to join the project, and Poul, Bruce, and Davin jointly built most of Greenfoot as it is today. All three are exceptional software developers, and their contribution to the project cannot be overstated. It is a joy working with them.

Eventually, the whole "BlueJ Group" got involved in the Greenfoot project, including John Rosenberg and Ian Utting, and this book builds on contributions and joint work of all group members.

Colleagues in the Computing Laboratory at the University of Kent also helped me a great deal, especially our Head of Department, Simon Thompson, who saw the value of Greenfoot early on and supported and encouraged its further development.

Another important contribution, without which the development of Greenfoot (and ultimately, this book) would not have been possible, is the generous support of Sun Microsystems. Emil Sarpa, Katherine Hartsell, Jessica Orquina, Sarah Hammond, and many others within Sun believed in the value of our system and provided important support.

Everyone at Pearson Education worked very hard to get this book published on time, with a very tight schedule, and in sometimes difficult circumstances. Tracy Dunkelberger worked with me on this book from the beginning. She managed amazingly well to stay positive and excited while putting up with my repeated missed deadlines, and she still encouraged me to continue writing. Melinda Haggerty did a whole lot of different things, including managing the reviews.

A special thank you needs to go to the reviewers of this book, who have provided very detailed, thoughtful, and useful feedback. They are Carolyn Oates, Damianne President, Detlef Rick, Gunnar Johannesmeyer, Josh Fishburn, Mark Hayes, Marla Parker, Matt Jadud, Todd O'Bryan, Lael Grant, Jason Green, Mark Lewis, Rodney Hoffman, and Michael Kadri. They helped spotting many errors and pointed out many opportunities for improvement.

My good friend Michael Caspersen also deserves thanks for providing early feedback and encouragement that was very important to me, partly because it helped improve the book, and more importantly because it encouraged me to believe that this work might be interesting to teachers and worthwhile completing.

# Introduction

Welcome to Greenfoot! In this book, we will discuss how to program graphical computer programs, such as simulations and games, using the Java Programming Language and the Greenfoot environment.

There are several goals in doing this: One is to learn programming, another is to have fun along the way. While the examples we discuss in this book are specific to the Greenfoot environment, the concepts are general: working through this book will teach you general programming principles in a modern, object-oriented programming language. However, it will also show you how to make your own computer game, a biology simulation, or an on-screen piano.

This book is very practically oriented. Chapters and exercises are structured around real, hands-on development tasks. First, there is a problem that we need to solve, then we look at language constructs and strategies that help us solve the problem. This is quite different from many introductory programming textbooks which are often structured around programming language constructs.

As a result, this book starts with less theory and more practical activity than most programming books. This is also the reason we use Greenfoot: It is the Greenfoot environment that makes this possible. Greenfoot allows us to play. And that does not only mean playing computer games; it means playing with programming: We can create objects, move them around on screen, call their methods, and observe what they do, all interactively and easily. This leads to a more hands-on approach to programming than what would be possible without such an environment.

A more practical approach does not mean that the book does not cover the necessary theory and principles as well. It's just that the order is changed. Instead of introducing a concept theoretically first, and then doing some exercises with it, we often jump right in and use a construct, initially explaining only as much as necessary to solve the task at hand, then come back to the theoretical background later. We typically follow a spiral approach: We introduce some aspects of a concept when we first encounter it, then revisit it later in another context, and gradually deepen our understanding.

The emphasis throughout is to make the work we do interesting, relevant, and enjoyable. There is no reason why computer programming has to be dry, formal, or boring. Having fun along the way is okay. We think we can manage making the experience interesting and pedagogically sound at the same time. This is an approach that has been called *serious fun*—we do something interesting, and learn something useful along the way.

This book can be used both as a self-study book and as a textbook in a programming course. Exercises are worked into the text throughout the book—if you do them all, you will come out of this as a fairly competent programmer.

The projects discussed in this book are easy enough that they can be managed by high school students, but they are also open and extendable enough that even seasoned programmers can find interesting and challenging aspects to do. While Greenfoot is an educational environment, Java is not a toy language. Since Java is our language of choice for this book, the projects discussed here (and others you may want to create in Greenfoot) can be made as complex and challenging as you like.

While it is possible to create simple games quickly and easily in Greenfoot, it is equally possible to build highly sophisticated simulations of complex systems, possibly using artificial intelligence algorithms, agent technology, database connectivity, or anything else you can think of. Java is a very rich language that opens the whole world of programming, and Greenfoot imposes no restrictions as to which aspects of the language you can use.

In other words, Greenfoot scales well. It allows easy entry for young beginners, but experienced programmers can also implement interesting, sophisticated scenarios.

You are limited only by your imagination.

# Getting to know Greenfoot

| | |
|---|---|
| **topics:** | the Greenfoot interface, interacting with objects, invoking methods, running a scenario |
| **concepts:** | object, class, method call, parameter, return value |

This book will show you how to develop computer games and simulations with Greenfoot, a development environment. In this chapter, we shall take a look at Greenfoot itself, see what it can do and how to use it. We do this by trying out some existing programs.

Once we are comfortable with using Greenfoot, we shall jump right into writing a game ourselves.

The best way to read this chapter (and indeed the whole book) is by sitting at your computer with Greenfoot open on your screen and the book open on your desk. We will regularly ask you to do things in Greenfoot while you read. Some of the tasks you can skip; however, you will have to do some in order to progress in the chapter. In any case, you will learn most if you follow along and do them.

At this stage, we assume that you have already installed the Greenfoot software and the book scenarios (described in Appendix A). If not, read through that appendix first.

## 1.1 Getting started

Start Greenfoot and open the scenario *leaves-and-wombats* from the *Greenfoot book scenarios* folder.

> **Note** If you are starting Greenfoot for the first time, you will see a dialog asking what you want to do. Click *Choose a scenario.* Otherwise, use *Scenario–Open*[1] from the menu.

---

[1] We use this notation to tell you to select functions from the menu. *Scenario–Open* refers to the *Open* item in the *Scenario* menu.

**Figure 1.1**
The Greenfoot main window

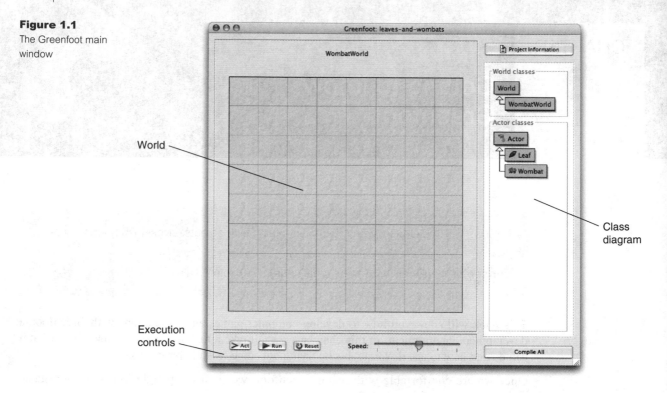

Make sure to open the *leaves-and-wombats* scenario that you find in the *book-scenarios* folder, not the somewhat similar *wombats* scenario from the standard Greenfoot installation.

You will now see the Greenfoot main window, with the scenario open, looking similar to Figure 1.1.

The main window consists of three main areas and a couple of extra buttons. The main areas are:

- The *world*. The largest area covering most of the screen (a sand-colored grid in this case) is called the world. This is where the program will run and we will see things happen.

- The *class diagram*. The area on the right with the beige-colored boxes and arrows is the class diagram. We shall discuss this in more detail shortly.

- The *execution controls*. The *Act*, *Run*, and *Reset* buttons and the speed slider at the bottom are the execution controls. We'll come back to them in a little while, too.

## 1.2 Objects and classes

We shall discuss the class diagram first. The class diagram shows us the classes involved in this scenario. In this case, they are `World`, `WombatWorld`, `Actor`, `Leaf`, and `Wombat`.

We shall be using the Java programming language for our projects. Java is an *object-oriented* language. The concepts of classes and objects are fundamental in object orientation.

Let us start by looking at the `Wombat` class. The class `Wombat` stands for the general concept of a wombat—it describes all wombats. Once we have a class in Greenfoot, we can create *objects* from it. (Objects are also often referred to as *instances* in programming—the two terms are synonyms.)

A wombat, by the way, is an Australian marsupial (Figure 1.2). If you want to find out more about them, do a Web search—it should give you plenty of results.

Right-click[2] on the Wombat class, and you will see the *class menu* pop up (Figure 1.3a). The first option in that menu, new Wombat(), lets us create new wombat objects. Try it out.

You will see that this gives you a small picture of a Wombat object, which you can move on screen with your mouse (Figure 1.3b). Place the *wombat* into the world by clicking anywhere in the world (Figure 1.3c).

**Figure 1.2**
A wombat in
Narawntapu National
Park, Tasmania[3]

**Figure 1.3**
a) The class menu.
b) Dragging a new
object.
c) Placing the object

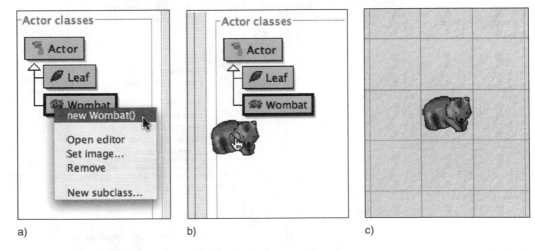

---

[2] On Mac OS, use ctrl-click instead of right-click if you have a one-button mouse.
[3] Image source: Wikipedia, subject to GNU Free Documentation License.

**Concept:**

Many **objects** can be created from a **class**.

Once you have a class in Greenfoot, you can create as many objects from it as you like.

**Exercise 1.1** Create some more wombats in the world. Create some leaves.

Currently, only the Wombat and Leaf classes are of interest to us. We shall discuss the other classes later.

## 1.3 Interacting with objects

Once we have placed some objects into the world, we can interact with these objects by right-clicking them. This will pop up the *object menu* (Figure 1.4). The object menu shows us all the operations this specific object can perform. For example, a wombat's object menu shows us what this wombat can do (plus two additional functions, *Inspect* and *Remove*, which we shall discuss later).

**Concept:**

Objects have **methods**. Invoking these performs an action.

In Java, these operations are called *methods*. It cannot hurt to get used to standard terminology straightaway, so we shall also call them methods from now on. We can *invoke* a method by selecting it from the menu.

**Exercise 1.2** Invoke the move() method on a wombat. What does it do? Try it several times. Invoke the turnLeft() method. Place two wombats into your world and make them face each other.

**Figure 1.4**
The wombat's *object menu*

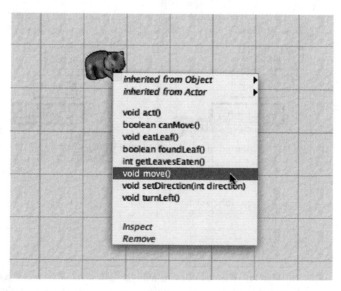

In short, we can start to make things happen by creating objects from one of the classes provided, and we can give commands to the objects by invoking their methods.

Let us have a closer look at the object menu. The move and turnLeft methods are listed as:

```
void move()
void turnLeft()
```

We can see that the method names are not the only things shown. There is also the word void at the beginning and a pair of parentheses at the end. These two cryptic bits of information tell us what data goes into the method call and what data comes back from it.

## 1.4 Return types

The word at the beginning is called the *return type*. It tells us what the method returns to us when we invoke it. The word void means "nothing" in this context: Methods with a void return type do not return any information. They just carry out their action, and then stop.

Any word other than void tells us that the method returns some information when invoked, and of what type that information is. In the wombat's menu (Figure 1.4) we can also see the words int and boolean. The word int is short for "integer" and refers to whole numbers (numbers without a decimal point). Examples of integer numbers are 3, 42, −3, and 12000000.

The type boolean has only two possible values: true and false. A method that returns a boolean will return either the value true or the value false to us.

Methods with void return types are like commands for our wombat. If we invoke the turnLeft method, the wombat obeys and turns left. Methods with non-void return types are like questions. Consider the canMove method:

```
boolean canMove()
```

When we invoke this method, we see a result similar to that shown in Figure 1.5, displayed in a dialog box. The important information here is the word true, which was returned by this

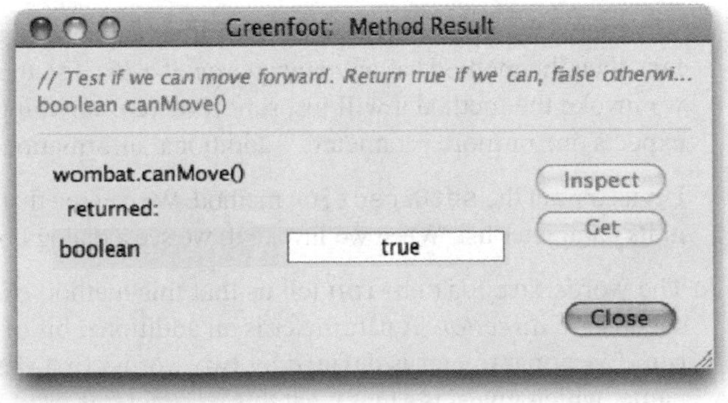

**Concept:**

The **return type** of a method specifies what a method call will return.

**Concept:**

A method with a **void** return type does not return a value.

**Figure 1.5**
A method result

method call. In effect, we have just asked the wombat "Can you move?" and the wombat has answered "Yes!" (`true`).

> **Exercise 1.3** Invoke the `canMove()` method on your wombat. Does it always return *true*? Or can you find situations in which it returns *false*?

Try out another method with a return value:

```
int getLeavesEaten()
```

Using this method, we can get the information how many leaves this wombat has eaten.

> **Exercise 1.4** Using a newly created wombat, the `getLeavesEaten()` method will always return zero. Can you create a situation in which the result of this method is not zero? (In other words: can you make your wombat eat some leaves?)

> **Concept:**
>
> Methods with void return types represent **commands**; methods with non-void return types represent **questions**.

Methods with non-void return types usually just tell us something about the object (*Can it move? How many leaves has it eaten?*), but do not change the object. The wombat is just as it was before we asked it about the leaves. Methods with `void` return types are usually commands to the objects that make it do something.

## 1.5 Parameters

The other bit in the *method* menu that we have not yet discussed are the parentheses after the method name.

```
int getLeavesEaten()
void setDirection(int direction)
```

> **Concept:**
>
> A **parameter** is a mechanism to pass in additional data to a method.

The parentheses after the method name hold the *parameter list*. This tells us whether the method requires any additional information to run, and if so, what kind of information.

If we see only a pair of parentheses without anything else within it (as we have in all methods so far), then the method has an *empty parameter list*. In other words, it expects no parameters—when we invoke the method it will just run. If there is anything within the parenthesis, then the method expects one or more parameters—additional information that we need to provide.

> **Concept:**
>
> Parameters and return values have **types**. Examples of types are int for numbers, and boolean for true/false values.

Let us try out the `setDirection` method. We can see that it has the words `int direction` written in its parameter list. When we invoke it, we see a dialog box similar to the one shown in Figure 1.6.

The words `int direction` tell us that this method expects one parameter of type `int`, which specifies a *direction*. A parameter is an additional bit of data we must provide for this method to run. Every parameter is defined by two words: first the parameter type (here: `int`) and then a name, which gives us a hint what this parameter is used for. If a method has a parameter, then we need to provide this additional information when we invoke the method.

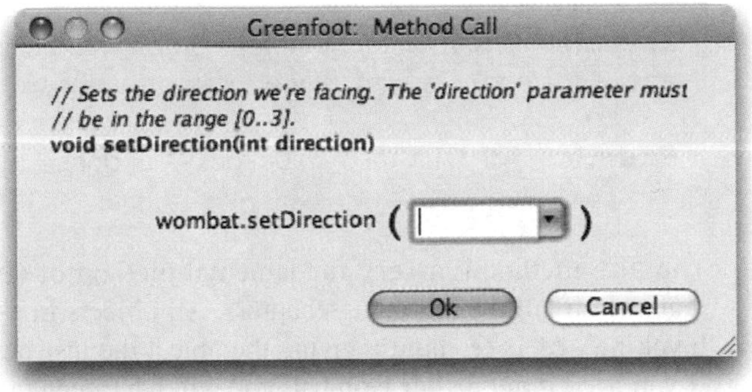

**Figure 1.6**
A method call dialog

In this case, the type int tells us that we now should provide a whole number, and the name suggests that this number somehow specifies the direction to turn to.

At the top of the dialog is a comment that tells us a little more: the direction parameter should be between 0 and 3.

**Exercise 1.5** Invoke the setDirection(int direction) method. Provide a parameter value and see what happens. Which number corresponds to which direction? Write them down. What happens when you type in a number greater than 3? What happens if you provide input that is not a whole number, such as a decimal number (2.5) or a word (three)?

The setDirection method expects only a single parameter. Later, we shall see cases where methods expect more than one parameter. In that case, the method will list all the parameters it expects within the parentheses.

The description of each method shown in the object menu, including the return type, method name, and parameter list, is called the *method signature*.

We have now reached a point where you can do the main interactions with Greenfoot objects. You can create objects from classes, interpret the method signatures, and invoke methods (with and without parameters).

**Concept:**

The specification of a method, which shows its return type, name, and parameters is called its **signature**.

## 1.6 Greenfoot execution

There is one other way of interacting with Greenfoot objects: the execution controls.

**Tip:**

You can place objects into the world more quickly by selecting a class in the class diagram, and then shift-clicking in the world.

**Exercise 1.6** Place a wombat and a good number of leaves into the world, and then invoke a wombat's act() method several times. What does this method do? How does it differ from the **move** method? Make sure to try different situations, for example, the wombat facing the edge of the world, or sitting on a leaf.

**Exercise 1.7** Still with a wombat and some leaves in the world, click the *Act* button in the execution controls near the bottom of the Greenfoot window. What does this do?

> **Exercise 1.8** What is the difference between clicking the *Act* button and invoking the `act()` method? (Try with several wombats in the world.)
>
> **Exercise 1.9** Click the *Run* button. What does it do?

The `act` method is a very fundamental method of Greenfoot objects. We shall encounter it regularly in all the following chapters. All objects in a Greenfoot world have this `act` method. Invoking `act` is essentially giving the object the instruction "Do whatever you want to do now". If you tried it out for our wombat, you will have seen that the wombat's `act` does something like the following:

- If we're sitting on a leaf, eat the leaf.

- Otherwise, if we can move forward, move forward.

- Otherwise, turn left.

> **Concept:**
>
> Objects that can be placed into the world are known as **actors**.

The experiments in the exercises above should also have shown you that the *Act* button in the execution controls simply calls the `act` method of the actors in the world. The only difference to invoking the method via the object menu is that the *Act* button invokes the `act` method of all objects in the world, whereas using the object menu affects only the one chosen object.

The *Run* button just calls `act` over and over again for all objects, until you click *Pause*.

Let us try out what we have discussed in the context of another scenario.

## 1.7 A second example

Open another scenario, named *asteroids1*, from the *chapter01* folder of the book scenarios. It should look similar to Figure 1.7 (except that you will not see the rocket or the asteroids on your screen yet).

## 1.8 Understanding the class diagram

Let us first have a closer look at the class diagram (Figure 1.8). At the top, you see the two classes called `World` and `Space`, connected by an arrow.

The `World` class is always there in all Greenfoot scenarios—it is built into Greenfoot. The class under it, `Space` in this case, represents the specific world for this particular scenario. Its name can be different in each scenario, but every scenario will have a specific world here.

> **Concept:**
>
> A **subclass** is a class that represents a specialization of another. In Greenfoot, this is shown with an arrow in the class diagram.

The arrow shows an *is-a* relationship: `Space` *is a* `World` (in the sense of Greenfoot worlds: `Space`, here, is a specific Greenfoot world). We also sometimes say that `Space` is a *subclass* of `World`.

We do not usually need to create objects of world classes—Greenfoot does that for us. When we open a scenario, Greenfoot automatically creates an object of the world subclass. The object is then shown on the main part of the screen. (The big black image of space is an object of the `Space` class.)

**Figure 1.7**
The asteroids1
scenario

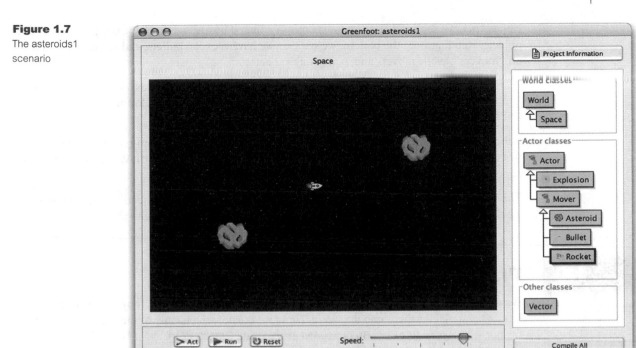

**Figure 1.8**
A class diagram

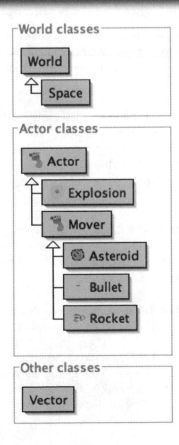

Below this, we see another group of six classes, linked by arrows. Each class represents its own objects. Reading from the bottom, we see that we have rockets, bullets, and asteroids, which are all "movers", while movers and explosions are actors.

Again, we have subclass relationships: Rocket, for example, is a subclass of Mover, and Mover and Explosion are subclasses of Actor. (Conversely, we say that Mover is a *superclass* of Rocket and Actor is a *superclass* of Explosion.)

Subclass relationships can go over several levels: Rocket, for example, is also a subclass of Actor (because it is a subclass of Mover, which is a subclass of Actor). We shall discuss more about the meaning of subclasses and superclasses later.

The class Vector, shown at the bottom of the diagram under the heading *Other classes* is a helper class used by the other classes. We cannot place objects of it into the world.

## 1.9 Playing with Asteroids

We can start playing with this scenario by creating some actor objects (objects of subclasses of Actor) and placing them into the world. Here, we create objects only of the classes that have no further subclasses: Rocket, Bullet, Asteroid, and Explosion.

Let us start by placing a rocket and two asteroids into space. (Remember: you can create objects by right-clicking on the class, or selecting the class and shift-clicking.)

When you have placed your objects, click the *Run* button. You can then control the spaceship with the arrow keys on your keyboard, and you can fire a shot by using the space bar. Try getting rid of the asteroids before you crash into them.

**Exercise 1.10** If you have played this game for a while, you will have noticed that you cannot fire very quickly. Let us tweak our spaceship firing software a bit so that we can shoot a bit quicker. (That should make getting the asteroids a bit easier!) Place a rocket into the world, then invoke its **setGunReloadTime** method (through the *object* menu), and set the reload time to 5. Play again (with at least two asteroids) to try it out.

**Exercise 1.11** Once you have managed to remove all asteroids (or at any other point in the game), stop the execution (press *Pause*) and find out how many shots you have fired. You can do this using a method from the rocket's object menu. (Try destroying two asteroids with as few shots as possible.)

**Exercise 1.12** You will have noticed that the rocket moves a bit as soon as you place it into the world. What is its initial speed?

**Exercise 1.13** Asteroids have an inherent *stability*. Each time they get hit by a bullet, their stability decreases. When it reaches zero, they break up. What is their initial stability value after you create them? By how much does the stability decrease from a single hit by a bullet?

(Hint: Just shoot an asteroid once, and then check the stability again. Another hint: To shoot the asteroid, you must run the game. To use the object menu, you must pause the game first.)

**Exercise 1.14** Make a very big asteroid.

# 1.10 Source code

**Concept:**

Every class is defined by **source code**. This code defines what objects of this class can do. We can look at the source code by opening the class's editor.

The behavior of each object is defined by its class. The way we can specify this behavior is by writing *source code* in the Java programming language. The source code of a class is the code that specifies all the details about the class and its objects. Selecting *Open editor* from the class's menu will show us an editor window (Figure 1.9) that contains the class's source code.

The source code for this class is fairly complex, and we do not need to understand it all at this stage. However, if you study the rest of this book and program your own games or simulations, you will learn over time how to write this code.

At this point, it is only important to understand that we can change the behavior of the objects by changing the class's source code. Let us try this out.

**Figure 1.9**
The editor window of class Rocket

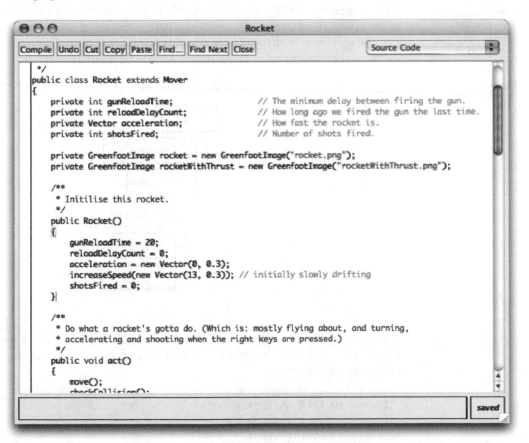

```
*/
public class Rocket extends Mover
{
    private int gunReloadTime;          // The minimum delay between firing the gun.
    private int reloadDelayCount;       // How long ago we fired the gun the last time.
    private Vector acceleration;        // How fast the rocket is.
    private int shotsFired;             // Number of shots fired.

    private GreenfootImage rocket = new GreenfootImage("rocket.png");
    private GreenfootImage rocketWithThrust = new GreenfootImage("rocketWithThrust.png");

    /**
     * Initialise this rocket.
     */
    public Rocket()
    {
        gunReloadTime = 20;
        reloadDelayCount = 0;
        acceleration = new Vector(0, 0.3);
        increaseSpeed(new Vector(13, 0.3)); // initially slowly drifting
        shotsFired = 0;
    }

    /**
     * Do what a rocket's gotta do. (Which is: mostly flying about, and turning,
     * accelerating and shooting when the right keys are pressed.)
     */
    public void act()
    {
        move();
        checkCollision();
```

We have seen before that the default firing speed of the rocket was fairly slow. We could change this for every rocket individually by invoking a method on each new rocket, but we would have to do this over and over again, every time we start playing. Instead, we can change the code of the rocket so that its initial firing speed is changed (say, to 5), so that all rockets in the future start with this improved behavior.

Open the editor for the `Rocket` class. About 25 lines from the top, you should find a line that reads

```
gunReloadTime = 20;
```

This is where the initial gun reloading time gets set. Change this line so that it reads

```
gunReloadTime = 5;
```

Be sure to change nothing else. You will notice very soon that programming systems are very picky. A single incorrect or missing character can lead to errors. If, for example, you remove the semicolon at the end of the line, you would run into an error fairly soon.

Close the editor window (our change is complete) and look at the class diagram again. It has now changed: Several classes now appear striped (Figure 1.10). The striped look indicates that a class has been edited and now must be *compiled*. Compilation is a translation process: The class's source code is translated into a machine code that your computer can execute.

Classes must always be compiled after their source code has been changed, before new objects of the class can be created. (You will also have noticed that several classes need recompilation even though we have changed only a single class. This is often the case because classes depend on each other. When one changes, several need to be translated again.)

**Figure 1.10**
Classes after editing

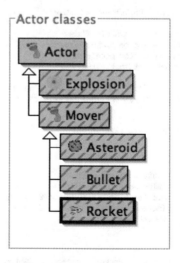

We can compile the classes by clicking the *Compile All* button in the bottom–right corner of Greenfoot's main window. Once the classes have been compiled, the stripes disappear, and we can create objects again.

**Exercise 1.15** Make the change to the `Rocket` class source code as described above. Close the editor and compile the classes. Try it out: rockets should now be able to fire quickly right from the start.

We shall come back to the asteroids game in Chapter 7, where we will discuss how to write this game.

## 1.11 Summary

In this chapter, we have seen what Greenfoot scenarios can look like and how to interact with them. We have seen how to create objects and how to communicate with these objects by invoking their methods. Some methods were commands to the object, while other methods returned information about the object. Parameters are used to provide additional information to methods, while return values pass information back to the caller.

Objects were created from their classes, and source code controls the definition of the class (and with this, the behavior and characteristics of all the class's objects).

We have seen that we can change the source code using an editor. After editing the source, classes need to be recompiled.

We will spend most of the rest of the book discussing how to write Java source code to create scenarios that do interesting things.

### Concept summary

- Greenfoot scenarios consist of a set of **classes**.

- Many **objects** can be created from a **class**.

- Objects have **methods**. Invoking these performs an action.

- The **return type** of a method specifies what a method call will return.

- A method with a **void** return type does not return a value.

- Methods with void return types represent **commands**; methods with non-void return types represent **questions**.

- A **parameter** is a mechanism to pass in additional data to a method.

- Parameters and return values have **types**. Examples of types are **int** for numbers, and **boolean** for true/false values.

- The specification of a method, which shows its return type, name, and parameters, is called its **signature**.

- Objects that can be placed into the world are known as **actors**.

- A **subclass** is a class that represents a specialization of another. In Greenfoot, this is shown with an arrow in the class diagram.

- Every class is defined by **source code**. This code defines what objects of this class can do. We can look at the source code by opening the class's editor.

- Computers do not understand source code. It needs to be translated to machine code before it can be executed. This is called **compilation**.

# The first program: Little Crab

| | |
|---|---|
| **topics:** | writing code: movement, turning, reacting to the screen edges |
| **concepts:** | source code, method call, parameter, sequence, if-statement |

In the previous chapter, we discussed how to use existing Greenfoot scenarios: We have created objects, invoked methods, and played a game.

Now, we shall start to make our own game.

## 2.1 The Little Crab scenario

The scenario we use for this chapter is called *little-crab*. You will find this scenario in the book projects for this book.

The scenario you see should look similar to Figure 2.1.

> **Exercise 2.1** Start Greenfoot and open the *little-crab* scenario. Place a crab into the world and run the program (click the *Run* button). What do you observe? (Remember: If the class icons on the right appear striped, you have to compile the project first.)

On the right, you see the classes in this scenario (Figure 2.2). We notice that there is the usual Greenfoot Actor class, a class called Animal, and the Crab class.

The hierarchy (denoted by the arrows) indicates an *is-a* relationship (also called *inheritance*): A crab *is an* animal, and an animal *is an* actor. (It follows then, that a crab also is an actor.)

Initially, we will work only with the Crab class. We will talk a little more about the Actor and Animal classes later on.

If you have done the exercise above, then you know the answer to the question "What do you observe?" It is: "nothing".

**Figure 2.1**
The *Little Crab*
scenario

**Figure 2.1**
The *Little Crab*
scenario

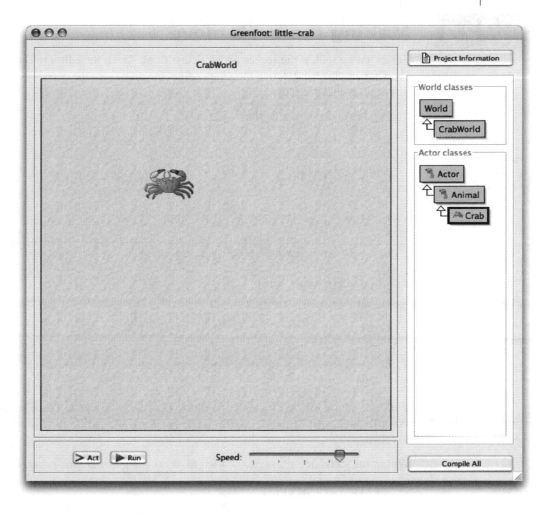

**Figure 2.2**
The *Little Crab* actor
classes

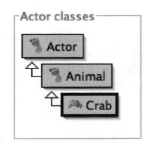

The crab does not do anything when Greenfoot runs. This is because there is no source code in the definition of the Crab class that specifies what the crab should do.

In this chapter, we shall work on changing this. The first thing we shall do is to make the crab move.

**2.2** # Making the crab move

Let us have a look at the source code of class `Crab`. Open the editor to display the `Crab` source. (You can do this by selecting the *Open editor* function from the class's popup menu, or you can just double-click the class.)

The source code you see is shown in Code 2.1.

**Code 2.1**

The original version of the `Crab` class

```
import greenfoot.*; // (World, Actor, GreenfootImage, and Greenfoot)

/**
 * This class defines a crab. Crabs live on the beach.
 */
public class Crab extends Animal
{
    public void act()
    {
        // Add your action code here.
    }
}
```

This is a standard Java class definition. That is, this text defines what the crab can do. We will look at it in detail a little later. For now, we will concentrate on getting the crab to move.

Within this class definition, we can see what is called the *act method*. It looks like this:

```
public void act()
{
    // Add your action code here.
}
```

The first line is the *signature* of the method. The last three lines—the two curly brackets and anything between them—is called the *body* of the method. Here, we can add some code that determines the actions of the crab. We can replace the gray text in the middle with a command. One such command is

```
move();
```

Note that it has to be written exactly as shown, including the parentheses and the semicolon. The `act` method should then look like this:

```
public void act()
{
    move();
}
```

> **Exercise 2.2** Change the `act` method in your crab class to include the `move()` instruction, as shown above. Compile the scenario (by clicking the *Compile All* button) and place a crab into the world. Try clicking the *Act* and *Run* buttons.
>
> **Exercise 2.3** Place multiple crabs into the world. Run the scenario. What do you observe?

**Concept:**

A **method call** is an instruction that tells an object to perform an action. The action is defined by a method of the object.

You will see that the crab can now move across the screen. The `move()` instruction makes the crab move a little bit to the right. When we click the *Act* button in the Greenfoot main window, the `act` method is executed once. That is, the instruction that we have written inside the `act` method (`move()`) executes.

Clicking the *Run* button is just like clicking the *Act* button several times, very quickly. So the `act` method is executed over and over again, until we click *Pause*.

**Terminology**

The instruction `move()` is called a **method call**. A **method** is an action that an object knows how to do (here, the object is the crab) and a **method call** is an instruction telling the crab to do it. The parentheses are part of the method call. Instructions like this end with a semicolon.

## 2.3 Turning

Let us see what other instructions we can use. The crab also understands a `turn` instruction. Here is what it looks like:

```
turn(5);
```

The number 5 in the instruction specifies how many degrees the crab should turn. This is called a *parameter*. We can also use other numbers, for example:

```
turn(23);
```

The degree value is specified out of 360 degrees, so any value between 0 and 359 can be used. (Turning 360 degrees would turn all the way around, so it is the same as turning 0 degrees, or not turning at all.)

**Concept:**

Additional information can be passed to some methods within the parentheses. The value passed is called a **parameter**.

If we want to turn instead of moving, we can replace the `move()` instruction with a `turn(5)` instruction. The `act` method then looks like this:

```
public void act()
{
    turn(5);
}
```

**Exercise 2.4** Replace `move()` with `turn(5)` in your scenario. Try it out. Also, try values other than 5 and see what it looks like. Remember: Every time you change your source code, you must compile again.

**Exercise 2.5** How can you make the crab turn left?

The next thing we can try is to both move and turn. The `act` method can hold more than one instruction—we can just write multiple instructions in a row.

Code 2.2 shows the complete `Crab` class, as it looks when we move and turn. In this case, at every act step, the crab will move and then turn (but these actions will happen so quickly after each other that it appears as if they happen at the same time).

**Code 2.2**

Making the crab move and turn

```java
import greenfoot.*; // (World, Actor, GreenfootImage, and Greenfoot)

/**
 * This class defines a crab. Crabs live on the beach.
 */
public class Crab extends Animal
{
    public void act()
    {
        move();
        turn(5);
    }
}
```

**Exercise 2.6** Use a `move()` and `turn(N)` instruction in your crab's `act` method. Try different values for *N*.

**Terminology**

The number within the parentheses in the `turn` instruction—that is, the 5 in `turn(5)`—is called a **parameter**. A parameter is an additional bit of information that we have to provide when we call some methods.

Some methods, like `move`, expect no parameters. They are happy to just execute as soon as we write the `move()` instruction. Other methods, such as `turn`, want more information: *How much should I turn?* In this case, we have to provide that information in the form of a parameter value within the parentheses, for instance, `turn(17)`.

## Side note: Errors

**Concept:**

When a class is compiled, the compiler checks to see whether there are any errors. If an error is found, an **error message** is displayed.

When we write source code, we have to be very careful—every single character counts. Getting one small thing wrong will result in our program not working. Usually, it will not compile.

This will happen to us regularly: When we write programs, we inevitably make mistakes, and then we have to correct them. Let us try that out now.

If, for example, we forget to write the semicolon after the move() instruction, we will be told about it when we try to compile.

> **Exercise 2.7** Open your editor to show the crab's source code, and remove the semicolon after move(). Then compile. Also experiment with other errors, such as misspelling **move** or making other random changes to the code. Make sure to change it all back after this exercise.
>
> **Exercise 2.8** Make various changes to cause different error messages. Find at least five different error messages. Write down each error message and what change you introduced to provoke this error.

**Tip:**

When an error message appears at the bottom of the editor window, a *question mark* button appears to the right of it. Clicking this button displays some additional information about the error message.

As we can see with this exercise, if we get one small detail wrong, Greenfoot will open the editor, highlight a line, and display a message at the bottom of the editor window. This message attempts to explain the error. The messages, however, vary considerably in their accuracy and usefulness. Sometimes they tell us fairly accurately what the problem is, but sometimes they are cryptic and hard to understand. The line that is highlighted is often the line where the problem is, but sometimes it is the line after the problem. When you see, for example, a "; expected" message, it is possible that the semicolon is in fact missing on the line above the highlighted line.

We will learn to read these messages a little better over time. For now, if you get a message and you are unsure what it means, look very carefully at your code and check that you have typed everything correctly.

## 2.4 Dealing with screen edges

When we made the crabs move and turn in the previous sections, they got stuck when they reached the edge of the screen. (Greenfoot is designed so that actors cannot leave the world and fall off its edge.)

Now, we shall improve this behavior so that the crab notices that it has reached the world edge and turns around. The question is, How can we do that?

Above, we have used the `move` and `turn` methods, so there might also be a method that helps us with our new goal. (In fact, there is.) But how do we find out what methods we have got available?

The `move` and `turn` methods we have used so far come from the `Animal` class. A crab is an animal (signified by the arrow that goes from `Crab` to `Animal` in the class diagram), therefore it can do whatever an animal can do. Our `Animal` class knows how to move and turn—that is why our crab can also do it. This is called *inheritance*: The `Crab` class inherits all the abilities (methods) from the `Animal` class.

The question now is, what else can our animals do?

To investigate this, we can open the editor for the `Animal` class. The editor can display two different views: It can show the source code (as we have seen for the `Crab` class) or it can show the documentation. The view can be switched using a popup selection menu in the top right corner of the editor window. We now want to look at the `Animal` class in the *Documentation view* (Figure 2.3).

**Figure 2.3**
Documentation view (with method summary) of the `Animal` class

Method summary

View switch

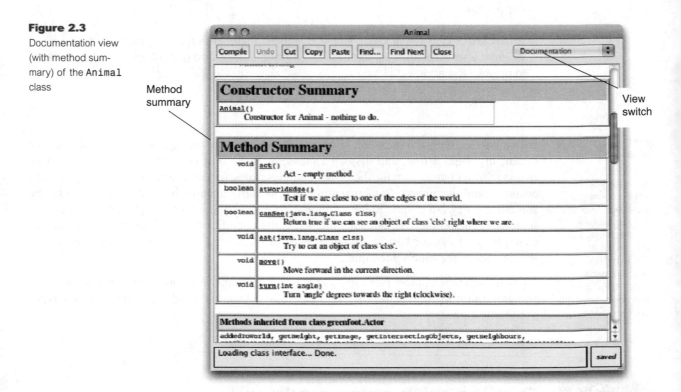

**Exercise 2.9** Open the editor for the **Animal** class. Switch to Documentation view. Find the list of methods for this class (the "Method Summary"). How many methods does this class have?

If we look at the method summary, we can see all the methods that the `Animal` class provides. Among them are three methods that are especially interesting to us at the moment. They are:

```
boolean atWorldEdge()
```
Test if we are close to one of the edges of the world.

```
void move()
```
Move forward in the current direction.

```
void turn(int angle)
```
Turn "angle" degrees toward the right (clockwise).

Here we see the signatures for three methods, as we first encountered them in Chapter 1. Each method signature starts with a return type and is followed by the method name and the parameter list. Below it, we see a comment describing what the method does. We can see that the three method names are `atWorldEdge`, `move`, and `turn`.

The `move` and `turn` methods are the ones we used in the previous sections. If we look at their parameter lists, we can see what we observed before: `move` has no parameters (the parentheses are empty), and `turn` expects one parameter of type `int` (a whole number) for the angle. (Read Section 1.5 again if you are unsure about parameter lists.)

We can also see that the `move` and `turn` methods have `void` as their return type. This means that neither method returns a value. We are commanding or instructing the object to move or to turn. The animal will just obey the command but not respond with an answer to us.

The signature for `atWorldEdge` is a little different. It is

```
boolean atWorldEdge()
```

This method has no parameters (there is nothing within the parentheses), but it specifies a return value: `boolean`. We have briefly encountered the `boolean` type in Section 1.4—it is a type that can hold two possible values: *true* or *false*.

Calling methods that have return values (where the return type is not `void`) is not like issuing a command, but asking a question. If we use the `atWorldEdge()` method, the method will respond with either `true` (Yes!) or `false` (No!). Thus, we can use this method to check whether we are at the edge of the world.

**Exercise 2.10** Create a crab. Right-click it, and find the `boolean atWorldEdge()` method (it is in the *inherited from Animal* submenu, since the crab inherited this method from the `Animal` class). Call this method. What does it return?

**Exercise 2.11** Let the crab run to the edge of the screen (or move it there manually), and then call the `atWorldEdge()` method again. What does it return now?

We can now combine this method with an *if-statement* to write the code shown in Code 2.3.

**Code 2.3**

Turning around at the edge of the world

```
import greenfoot.*; // (World, Actor, GreenfootImage, and Greenfoot)

/**
 * This class defines a crab. Crabs live on the beach.
 */
public class Crab extends Animal
{
    public void act()
    {
        if ( atWorldEdge() )
        {
            turn(17);
        }
        move();
    }
}
```

**Concept:**

An **if-statement** can be used to write instructions that are executed only when a certain condition is true.

The if-statement is a part of the Java language that makes it possible to execute commands only if some condition is true. For example, here we want to turn only if we are near the edge of the world. The code we have written is:

```
if ( atWorldEdge() )
{
    turn(17);
}
move();
```

The general form of an if-statement is this:

```
if ( condition )
{
    instruction;
    instruction;
    ...
}
```

In place of the *condition* can be any expression that is either true or false (such as our `atWorldEdge()` method call), and the *instructions* will be executed only if the condition is true. There can be one or more instructions.

If the condition is false, the instructions are just skipped, and execution continues under the closing curly bracket of the if-statement.

Note that our `move()` method call is outside the if-statement, so it will be executed in any case. In other words: If we are at the edge of the world, we turn and then move; if we are not at the edge of the world, we just move.

**Tip:**

In the Greenfoot editor, when you place the cursor behind an opening or closing bracket, Greenfoot will mark the matching closing or opening bracket. This can be used to check whether your brackets match up as they should.

**Exercise 2.12** Try it out! Type in the code discussed above and see if you can make your crabs turn at the edge of the screen. Pay close attention to the opening and closing brackets—it is easy to miss one or have too many.

**Exercise 2.13** Experiment with different values for the parameter to the `turn` method. Find one that looks good.

**Exercise 2.14** Place the `move()` statement inside the if-statement, rather than after it. Find out what is the effect and explain the behavior you observe. (Then, fix it again by moving it back where it was.)

**Note: Indentation**

In all the code examples you have seen so far (for instance, Code 2.3), you may have noticed some careful indentation being used. Every time a curly bracket opens, the following lines are indented one level more than the previous ones. When a curly bracket closes, the indentation goes back one level, so that the closing curly bracket is directly below the matching opening bracket. This makes it easy to find the matching bracket.

We use four spaces for one level of indentation. The Tab key will insert spaces in your editor for one level of indentation as well.

Taking care with indentation in your own code is very important. If you do not indent carefully, some errors (particularly misplaced or mismatched curly brackets) are very hard to spot. Proper indentation makes code much easier to read, and thus avoid potential errors.

## 2.5 Summary of programming techniques

In this book, we are discussing programming from a very example-driven perspective. We introduce general programming techniques as we need them to improve our scenarios. We shall summarize the important programming techniques at the end of each chapter to make it clear what you really need to take away from the discussion in order to progress well.

In this chapter, we have seen how to call methods (such as `move()`), with and without parameters. This will form the basis for all further Java programming. We have also learnt to identify the body of the `act` method—this is where we start writing our instructions.

You have encountered some error messages. This will continue throughout all your programming endeavors. We all make mistakes, and we all encounter error messages. This is not a sign of a bad programmer—it is a normal part of programming.

We have encountered a first glimpse of inheritance: Classes inherit the methods from their superclasses. The Documentation view of a class gives us a summary of the methods available.

And, very importantly, we have seen how to make decisions: We have used an if-statement for conditional execution. This went hand in hand with the appearance of the type `boolean`, a value that can be *true* or *false*.

## Concept summary

- A **method call** is an instruction that tells an object to perform an action. The action is defined by a method of the object.

- Additional information can be passed to some methods within the parentheses. The value passed is called a **parameter**.

- Multiple instructions are executed **in sequence**, one after the other, in the order in which they are written.

- When a class is compiled, the compiler checks to see whether there are any errors. If an error is found, an **error message** is displayed.

- A subclass **inherits** all the methods from its superclass. That means that it has, and can use, all methods that its superclass defines.

- Calling a method with a **void return type** issues a command. Calling a method with a **non-void return type** asks a question.

- An **if-statement** can be used to write instructions that are executed only when a certain condition is true.

# Improving the Crab—more sophisticated programming

| | |
|---|---|
| **topics:** | random behavior, keyboard control, sound |
| **concepts:** | dot notation, random numbers, defining methods, comments |

In the previous chapter, we looked at the basics of starting to program our first game. There were many new things that we had to look at. Now, we will add more interesting behavior. Adding code will get a little easier from now on, since we have seen many of the fundamental concepts.

The first thing we shall look at is adding some random behavior.

## 3.1 Adding random behavior

In our current implementation, the crab can walk across the screen, and it can turn at the edge of our world. But when it walks, it always walks exactly straight. That is what we want to change now. Crabs don't always go in an exact straight line, so let us add a little random behavior: The crab should go roughly straight, but every now and then it should turn a little off course.

We can achieve this in Greenfoot by using random numbers. The Greenfoot environment itself has a method to give us a random number. This method, called `getRandomNumber`, expects a parameter that specifies the limit of the number. It will then return a random number between 0 (zero) and the limit. For example,

```
Greenfoot.getRandomNumber(20)
```

will give us a random number between 0 and 20. The limit—20—is excluded, so the number is actually in the range 0–19.

The notation used here is called *dot notation*. When we called methods that were defined in our own class or inherited, it was enough to write the method name and parameter list. When the method is defined in another class, we need to specify the class or object that has the method, followed by a period (dot), followed by the method name and parameter. Since the `getRandomNumber` method is not in the `Crab` or `Animal` class, but in a class called `Greenfoot`, we have to write "`Greenfoot.`" in front of the method call.

**Concept:**

When a method we wish to call is not in our own class or inherited, we need to specify the class or object that has the method before the method name, followed by a dot. This is called **dot notation**.

**Concept:**

Methods that belong to classes (as opposed to objects) are marked with the keyword **static** in their signature. They are also called **class methods**.

### Note: Static methods

Methods may belong to objects or classes. When methods belong to a class, we write

```
class-name.method-name (parameters);
```

to call the method. When a method belongs to an object, we write

```
object.method-name (parameters);
```

to call it.

Both kinds of methods are defined in a class. The method signature tells us whether a given method belongs to objects of that class, or to the class itself.

Methods that belong to the class itself are marked with the keyword **static** at the beginning of the method signature. For example, the signature of Greenfoot's `getRandomNumber` method is

```
static int getRandomNumber(int limit);
```

This tells us that we must write the name of the class itself (Greenfoot) before the dot in the method call.

We will encounter calls to methods that belong to other objects in a later chapter.

Let us say we want to program our crab so that there is a 10 percent chance at every step that the crab turns a little bit off course. We can do the main part of this with an if-statement:

```
if ( something-is-true )
{
    turn(5);
}
```

Now we have to find an expression to put in place of *something-is-true* that returns true in exactly 10 percent of the cases.

We can do this using a random number (using the `Greenfoot.getRandomNumber` method) and a less-than operator. The less-than operator compares two numbers and returns true if the first is less than the second. "Less than" is written using the symbol "<". For example:

```
2 < 33
```

is true, while

```
162 < 42
```

is false.

**Exercise 3.1** Before reading on, try to write down, on paper, an expression using the `getRandomNumber` method and the less-than operator that, when executed, is true exactly 10 percent of the time.

**Exercise 3.2** Write down another expression that is true 7 percent of the time.

If we want to express the chance in percent, it is easiest to deal with random numbers out of 100. An expression that is true 10 percent of the time, for example, could be

```
Greenfoot.getRandomNumber(100) < 10
```

Since the call to `Greenfoot.getRandomNumber(100)` gives us a new random number between 0 and 99 every time we call it, and since these numbers are evenly distributed, they will be below 10 in 10 percent of all cases.

We can now use this to make our crab turn a little in 10 percent of its steps (Code 3.1).

**Code 3.1**

Random course changes—first try

```
import greenfoot.*; // (World, Actor, GreenfootImage, and Greenfoot)

/**
 * This class defines a crab. Crabs live on the beach.
 */
public class Crab extends Animal
{
    public void act()
    {
        if ( atWorldEdge() )
        {
            turn(17);
        }

        if ( Greenfoot.getRandomNumber(100) < 10 )
        {
            turn(5);
        }

        move();
    }
}
```

**Exercise 3.3** Try out the random course changes shown above in your own version. Experiment with different probabilities for turning.

This is a pretty good start, but it is not quite nice yet. First of all, if the crab turns, it always turns the same amount (5 degrees), and secondly, it always turns right, never left. What we would really like to see is that the crab turns a small, but random amount to either its left or its right. (We will discuss this now. If you feel confident enough, try to implement this on your own first before reading on.)

The simple trick to the first problem—always turning the same amount, in our case 5 degrees— is to replace the fixed number 5 in our code with another random number, like this:

```
if ( Greenfoot.getRandomNumber(100) < 10 )
{
    turn( Greenfoot.getRandomNumber(45) );
}
```

In this example, the crab still turns in 10 percent of its steps. And when it turns, it will turn a random amount, between 0 and 44 degrees.

**Exercise 3.4** Try out the code shown above. What do you observe? Does the crab turn different amounts when it turns?

**Exercise 3.5** We still have the problem that the crab turns only right. That's not normal behavior for a crab, so let's fix this. Modify your code so that the crab turns either right or left by up to 45 degrees each time it turns.

**Exercise 3.6** Try running your scenario with multiple crabs in the world. Do they all turn at the same time, or independently? Why?

The project *little-crab-2* (included in the book scenarios) shows an implementation of what we have done so far, including the last exercises.

## 3.2 Adding worms

Let us make our world a little more interesting by adding another kind of animal.

Crabs like to eat worms. (Well, that is not true for all kinds of crab in the real world, but there are some that do. Let's just say our crab is one of those that like to eat worms.) So let us now add a class for worms.

We can add new actor classes to a Greenfoot scenario by selecting *New subclass* from one of the existing actor classes (Figure 3.1). In this case, our new class Worm is a specific kind of animal, so it should be a subclass of class Animal. (Remember, being a subclass is an *is-a* relationship: A worm *is an* animal.)

When we are creating a new subclass, we are prompted to enter a name for the class and to select an image (Figure 3.2).

In our case, we name the class "Worm". By convention, class names in Java should always start with a capital letter. They should also describe what kind of object they represent, so "Worm" is the obvious name for our purpose.

Then, we should assign an image to the class. There are some images associated with the scenario, and a whole library of generic images to choose from. In this case, we have prepared a worm image and made it available in the scenario images, so we can just select the image named *worm.png*.

**Figure 3.1**
Creating new
subclasses

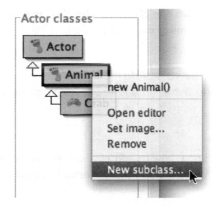

**Figure 3.2**
Creating a new class

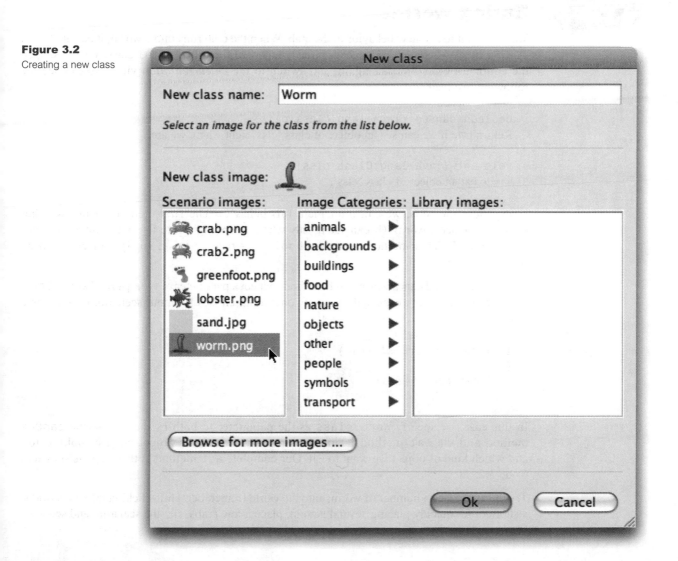

Once done, we can click *Ok*. The class is now added to our scenario, and we can compile and then add worms to our world.

> **Exercise 3.7** Add some worms to your world. Also add some crabs. Run the scenario. What do you observe? What do the worms do? What happens when a crab meets a worm?

We now know how to add new classes to our scenario. The next task is to make these classes interact: When a crab finds a worm, it should eat it.

## 3.3 Eating worms

We now want to add new behavior to the crab: When the crab runs into a worm, it eats it. Again, we first check what methods we have already inherited from the `Animal` class. When we open the editor for class `Animal` again, and switch to the *Documentation* view, we can see the following two methods:

```
boolean canSee (java.lang.Class clss)
```
Return true if we can see an object of class 'clss' right where we are.

```
void eat (java.lang.Class clss)
```
Try to eat an object of class 'clss'.

Using these methods, we can implement this behavior. The first method checks whether the crab can see a worm. (It can see it only when it runs right into it—our animals are very short-sighted.) This method returns a `boolean`—*true* or *false*, so we can use it in an if-statement.

The second method eats a worm. Both methods expect a parameter of type `java.lang.Class`. This means that we are expected to specify one of our classes from our scenario. Here is some sample code:

```
if ( canSee(Worm.class) )
{
    eat(Worm.class);
}
```

In this case, we specify `Worm.class` as the parameter to both method calls (the `canSee` method and the `eat` method). This declares which kind of object we are looking for, and which kind of object we want to eat. Our complete `act` method at this stage is shown in Code 3.2.

Try this out. Place a number of worms into the world (remember: shift-clicking into the world is a shortcut for quickly placing several actors), place a few crabs, run the scenario, and see what happens.

**Code 3.2**

First version of eating
a worm

```java
public void act()
{
    if ( atWorldEdge() )
    [
        turn(17);
    }

    if ( Greenfoot.getRandomNumber(100) < 10 )
    {
        turn(Greenfoot.getRandomNumber(90)−45);
    }
    move();

    if ( canSee(Worm.class) )
    {
        eat(Worm.class);
    }
}
```

**Advanced note: Packages**

*(The notes labeled "Advanced note" are inserted for deeper information for those readers really interested in the details. They are not crucial to understand at this stage, and could safely be skipped.)*

In the definition of the `canSee` and `eat` methods, we have seen a parameter type with the name `java.lang.Class`. What is going on here?

Many types are defined by classes. Many of those classes are in the standard Java class library. You can see the documentation of the Java class library by choosing *Java Library Documentation* from Greenfoot's *Help* menu.

The Java class library contains thousands of classes. To make these a little easier to work with, they have been grouped into *packages* (logically related groups of classes). When a class name includes dots, such as `java.lang.Class,` only the last part is the name of the class itself, and the former parts form the name of the package. So here we are looking at the class named "Class" from the package "java.lang".

Try to find that class in the Java library documentation.

## 3.4 Creating new methods

In the previous few sections, we have added new behavior to the crab—turning at the edge of the world, occasional random turns, and eating worms. If we continue to do this in the way we have done so far, the `act` method will become longer and longer, and eventually really hard to understand. We can improve this by chopping it up into smaller pieces.

**Concept:**

A **method defini-
tion** defines a new
action for objects
of this class. The
action is not imme-
diately executed,
but the method
can be called with
a method call later
to execute it.

We can create our own additional methods in the Crab class for our own purposes. For example, instead of just writing some code that looks for a worm and eats it into the act method, we
can add a new method for this purpose. To do this, we first have to decide on a name for this
method. Let us say we call it lookForWorm. We can then create a new method by adding the
following code:

```
/**
 * Check whether we have stumbled upon a worm.
 * If we have, eat it. If not, do nothing.
 */
public void lookForWorm()
{
    if ( canSee(Worm.class) )
    {
        eat(Worm.class);
    }
}
```

**Concept:**

**Comments** are
written into the
source code as
explanations for
human readers.
They are ignored
by the computer.

The first four lines are a *comment*. A comment is ignored by the computer—it is written for
human readers. We use a comment to explain to other human readers what the purpose of this
method is.

When we define this method, the code does not immediately get executed. In fact, by just defining
this method, it does not get executed at all. We are just defining a new possible action ("looking for
a worm") that can be carried out later. It will only be carried out when this method is called. We
can add a call to this method inside the act method:

```
lookForWorm();
```

Note that the call has the parentheses for the (empty) parameter list. The complete source code
after this restructuring is shown in Code 3.3.

**Code 3.3**

Splitting code into
separate methods

```
public void act()
{
    if ( atWorldEdge() )
    {
        turn(17);
    }

    if ( Greenfoot.getRandomNumber(100) < 10 )
    {
        turn(5);
    }

    move();
    lookForWorm();
}
```

**Code 3.3 continued**

Splitting code into separate methods

```java
/**
 * Check whether we have stumbled upon a worm.
 * If we have, eat it. If not, do nothing.
 */
public void lookForWorm()
{
    if ( canSee(Worm.class) )
    {
        eat(Worm.class);
    }
}
```

Note that this code change does not change the behavior of our crab at all. It just makes the code easier to read in the long run. As we add more code to the class, methods tend to become longer and longer. Longer methods are harder to understand. By separating our code into a number of shorter methods, we make the code easier to read.

**Exercise 3.8** Create another new method named `randomTurn` (this method has no parameters and returns nothing). Select the code that does the random turning, and move it from the `act` method to the `randomTurn` method. Then call this new `randomTurn` method from your `act` method. Make sure to write a comment for this method.

**Exercise 3.9** Create yet another method named `turnAtEdge` (it also has no parameters and returns nothing). Move the code that checks whether we are at the edge of the world (and does the turn if we are) into the `turnAtEdge` method. Call the `turnAtEdge` method from your `act` method. Your `act` method should now look like the version shown in Code 3.4.

**Code 3.4**

The new act method after creating methods for the subtasks

```java
public void act()
{
    turnAtEdge();
    randomTurn();
    move();
    lookForWorm();
}
```

By convention, method names in Java always start with a lowercase letter. Method names cannot contain spaces (or many other punctuation characters). If the method name logically consists of multiple words, we use capitals in the middle of the method name to mark the start of each word.

## 3.5 Adding a Lobster

We are now at a stage where we have a crab that walks more or less randomly through our world, and eats worms if it happens to run into them.

To make it a little more interesting, let us add another creature: a lobster.

Lobsters, in our scenario, like to chase crabs.

> **Exercise 3.10** Add a new class to your scenario. The class should be a subclass of `Animal`, called `Lobster` (with a capital 'L'), and it should use the prepared image *lobster.png*.
>
> **Exercise 3.11** What do you expect lobsters to do when you place them into the world as they are? Compile your scenario and try it out.

We now want to program our new lobsters to eat crabs. This is quite easy to do, since the behavior is very similar to the behavior of crabs. The only difference is that lobsters look for crabs, while crabs look for worms.

> **Exercise 3.12** Copy the complete `act` method from the `Crab` class into the `Lobster` class. Also copy the complete `lookForWorm`, `turnAtEdge`, and `randomTurn` methods.
>
> **Exercise 3.13** Change the `Lobster` code so that it looks for crabs, rather than worms. You can do that by changing every occurrence of "Worm" in the source code to "Crab". For instance, where `Worm.class` is mentioned, change it to `Crab.class`. Also change the name `lookForWorm` to `lookForCrab`. Make sure to update your comments.
>
> **Exercise 3.14** Place a crab, three lobsters, and many worms into the world. Run the scenario. Does the crab manage to eat all worms before it is caught by a lobster?

You should now have a version of your scenario where both crabs and lobsters walk around randomly, looking for worms and crabs, respectively.

Now, let us turn this program into a game.

## 3.6 Keyboard control

To get game-like behavior, we need to get a player involved. The player (you!) should be able to control the crab with the keyboard, while the lobsters continue to run randomly by themselves, as they already do.

The Greenfoot environment has a method that lets us check whether a key on the keyboard has been pressed. It is called `isKeyDown`, and, like the `getRandomNumber` method that we encountered in section 3.1, it is a method in the `Greenfoot` class. The method signature is

```
static boolean isKeyDown(String key)
```

We can see that the method is static (it is a class method) and the return type is `boolean`. This means that the method returns either *true* or *false*, and can be used as a condition in an if-statement.

We also see that the method expects a parameter of type `String`. A `String` is a piece of text (such as a word or a sentence), written in double quotes. The following are examples of `Strings`:

```
"This is a String"
"name"
"A"
```

In this case, the `String` expected is the name of the key that we want to test. Every key on the keyboard has a name. For those keys that produce visible characters, that character is their name, for example, the A-key is called "A". Other keys have names too. For instance, the left cursor key is called "left". Thus, if we want to test whether the left cursor key has been pressed, we can write

```
if (Greenfoot.isKeyDown("left"))
{
    ...// do something
}
```

Note that we need to write "Greenfoot." in front of the call to `isKeyDown`, since this method is defined in the `Greenfoot` class.

**Tip:**

Greenfoot automatically saves classes and scenarios when their windows are closed. To keep a copy of interim stages of scenarios, use **Save A Copy As** from the Scenario menu.

If, for example, we want our crab to turn left by 4 degrees whenever the left cursor key is being pressed, we can write

```
if (Greenfoot.isKeyDown("left"))
{
        turn(-4);
}
```

The idea now is to remove the code from the crab that does the random turning and also the code that turns automatically at the world edge and replace them with the code that lets us control the crab's turn with our keyboard.

**Exercise 3.15** Remove the random turning code from the crab.

**Exercise 3.16** Remove the code from the crab that does the turn at the edge of the world.

**Exercise 3.17** Add code into the crab's **act** method that makes the crab turn left whenever the left cursor key is pressed. Test.

**Exercise 3.18** Add another—similar—bit of code to the crab's **act** method that makes the crab turn right whenever the right cursor key is pressed.

**Exercise 3.19** If you have not done so in the first place, make sure that the code that checks the key-presses and does the turning is not written directly in the act method, but is instead in a separate method, maybe called **checkKeypress**. This method should be called from the **act** method.

Try solving the tasks by yourself first. If you get stuck, have a look on the next page. Code 3.5 shows the crab's complete act and `checkKeypress` methods after this change. The solution is also available in the book scenarios, as *little-crab-3*. This version includes all the changes we have discussed so far.

**Code 3.5**

The Crab's "act" method: Controlling the crab with the keyboard

```
/**
 * Act - do whatever the crab wants to do.
 */
public void act()
{
    checkKeypress();
    move();
    lookForWorm();
}


/**
 * Check whether a control key on the keyboard has been pressed.
 * If it has, react accordingly.
 */
public void checkKeypress()
{
    if (Greenfoot.isKeyDown("left"))
    {
        turn(-4);
    }
    if (Greenfoot.isKeyDown("right"))
    {
        turn(4);
    }
}
```

You are now ready to have a first try at playing your game! Place a crab, some worms, and a few lobsters into the world, and see whether you can get all the worms before the lobsters catch you. (Obviously, the more lobsters you place, the harder it gets...)

## 3.7 Ending the game

One simple improvement we can make is to end execution of the game when the crab is caught by a lobster. Greenfoot has a method to do this—we just need to find out what it is called.

To find out what the available methods in Greenfoot are, we can look at the documentation of the Greenfoot classes.

**Concept:**

The **API Documentation** lists all classes and methods available in Greenfoot. We often need to look up methods here.

In Greenfoot, choose *Greenfoot Class Documentation* from the *Help* menu. This will show the documentation for all the Greenfoot classes in a Web browser (Figure 3.3).

This documentation is also called the *Greenfoot API* (for application programmers' interface). The API shows all available classes and, for each class, all the available methods. You can see that Greenfoot offers five classes: `Actor`, `Greenfoot`, `GreenfootImage`, `MouseInfo`, and `World`.

**Figure 3.3**
The Greenfoot API in
a browser window

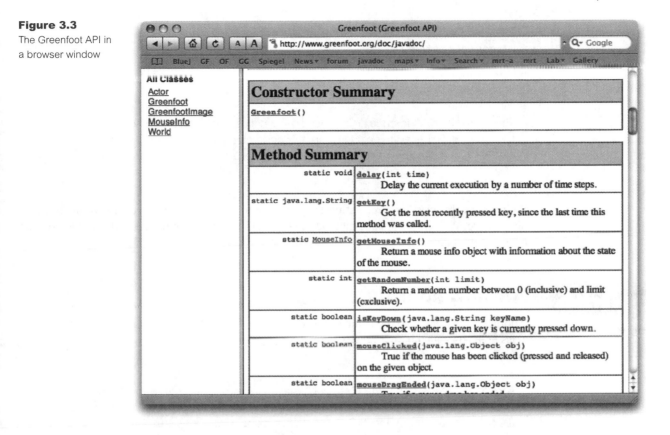

The method we are looking for is in the `Greenfoot` class.

**Exercise 3.20** Open the Greenfoot API in your browser. Select the `Greenfoot` class. In its documentation, find the section titled "Method Summary". In this section, try to find a method that stops the execution of the running scenario. What is this method called?

**Exercise 3.21** Does this method expect any parameters? What is its return type?

We can see the documentation of the Greenfoot classes by selecting them in the list on the left. For each class, the main panel in the browser displays a general comment, details of its constructors, and a list of its methods. (Constructors will be discussed in a later chapter.)

If we browse through the list of available methods in the class `Greenfoot`, we can find a method named `stop`. This is the method that we can use to stop execution when the crab gets caught.

We can make use of this method by writing

```
Greenfoot.stop();
```

into our source code.

> **Exercise 3.22** Add code to your own scenario that stops the game when a lobster catches the crab. You will need to decide where this code needs to be added. Find the place in your code that gets executed when a lobster eats a crab, and add this line of code there.

We will use this class documentation frequently in the future to look up details of methods we need to use. We will know some methods by heart after a while, but there are always methods we need to look up.

## 3.8    Adding sound

Another improvement to our game is the addition of sounds. Again, a method in the `Greenfoot` class helps us with this.

> **Exercise 3.23** Open the *Greenfoot Class Documentation* (from the *Help* menu), and look at the documentation of class `Greenfoot`. Find the details of the method that can be used to play a sound. What is its name? What parameters does it expect?

By looking through the documentation, we can see that the `Greenfoot` class has a method called `playSound`. It expects the name of a sound file (as String) as a parameter, and returns nothing.

> **Note**
>
> You may like to look at the structure of a Greenfoot scenario in your file system. If you look into the folder containing the book scenarios, you can find a folder for each Greenfoot scenario. For the crab example, there are several different versions (*little-crab*, *little-clab-2*, *little-crab-3*, etc.). Inside each scenario folder are several files for each scenario class, and several other support files. There are also two media folders: *images* holds the scenario images and *sounds* stores the sound files.
>
> You can see the available sounds by looking into this folder, and you can make more sounds available by storing them here.

In our crab scenario, two sound files are already included. They are called *slurp.wav* and *au.wav*.

We can now easily play one of the sounds by using the following method call:

```
Greenfoot.playSound("slurp.wav");
```

Try it out!

> **Exercise 3.24** Add playing of sounds to your scenario: When a crab eats a worm, play the "slurp.wav" sound. When a lobster eats the crab, play the "au.wav" sound. To do this, you have to find the place in your code where this should happen.

The *little-crab-4* version of this scenario shows the solution to this. It is a version of the project that includes all the functionality we have discussed so far: worms, lobsters, keyboard control, and sound (Figure 3.4).

**Figure 3.4**
The crab game with worms and lobsters

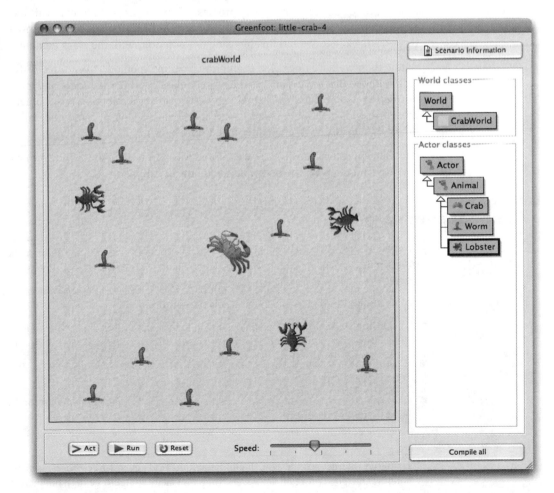

**About sound recording**

You can also make your own sounds. Both the sounds included are recorded by simply speaking into the computer's microphone. Use one of the many free sound recording programs[1], record your sound, and save (or export) it as a sound file, in either WAV, AIFF, or AU format. Making your own sounds is further discussed in Chapter 8.

**Exercise 3.25** If you have a microphone on your computer, make your own sounds to use when the worms or the crab get eaten. Record the sounds with any sound recording program, store them in the scenario's *sounds* folder, and use them in your code.

## 3.9 Summary of programming techniques

In this chapter we have seen more examples of using an if-statement—this time for turning at random times and reacting to key presses. We have also seen how to call methods from another class, namely the `getRandomNumber`, `isKeyDown`, and `playSound` methods from the `Greenfoot` class. We did this by using dot notation, with the class name in front of the dot.

Altogether, we have now seen examples of calling methods from three different places. We can call methods that are defined in the current class itself (called *local methods*), method that were defined in a superclass (*inherited methods*), and static methods from other classes. The last of these uses dot notation. (There is one additional version of a method call: calling methods on other objects—we will encounter that a little later.)

Another important aspect that we explored was how to read the API documentation of an existing class to find out what methods it has and how to call them.

**Concept summary**

- When a method we wish to call is not in our own class or inherited, we need to specify the class or object that has the method before the method name, followed by a dot. This is called **dot notation**.

- Methods that belong to classes (as opposed to objects) are marked with the keyword **static** in their signature. They are also called **class methods**.

- A **method definition** defines a new action for objects of this class. The action is not immediately executed, but the method can be called with a method call later to execute it.

- **Comments** are written into the source code as explanations for human readers. They are ignored by the computer.

- The **API Documentation** lists all classes and methods available in Greenfoot. We often need to look up methods here.

---

[1] Using an Internet search, you should be able to find several free programs that can record and save sounds. One good program is *Audacity* (http://audacity.sourceforge.net), but there are many others.

# Finishing the crab game

| | |
|---|---|
| **topics:** | world initialization, setting images, animating images |
| **concepts:** | constructors, state, instance variables (fields), assignment, new (creating objects programmatically) |

In this chapter, we will finish the crab game. "Finish" here means that this is where we stop discussing this project in this book. Of course, a game is never finished—you can always think of more improvements that you can add. We will suggest some ideas at the end of this chapter. First, however, we will discuss a number of improvements in detail.

## 4.1 Adding objects automatically

We are now getting close to having a playable little game. However, a few more things need to be done. The first problem that should be addressed is the fact that we always have to place the actors (the crab, lobsters, and worms) manually into the world. It would be better if that happened automatically.

There is one thing that happens automatically every time we successfully compile: The world itself is created. The world object, as we see it on screen (the sand-colored square area), is an instance of the CrabWorld class. World instances are treated in a special way in Greenfoot: While we have to create instances of our actors ourselves, the Greenfoot system always automatically creates one instance of our world class and displays that instance on screen.

Let us have a look at the CrabWorld's source code (Code 4.1). (If you do not have your own crab game at this stage, use *little-crab-4* for this chapter.)

In this class, we see the usual import statement in the first line. (We will discuss this statement in detail later—for now it is enough to know that this line will always appear at the top of our Greenfoot classes.)

Then follows the class header, and a comment (the block of lines in a blue-ish color starting with asterisks—we have encountered them already in the last chapter). Comments usually start with a /** symbol and end with */.

**Code 4.1**

Source code of the
`CrabWorld` class

```
import greenfoot.*; // (Actor, World, Greenfoot, GreenfootImage)

public class CrabWorld extends World
{
    /**
     * Create the crab world (the beach). Our world has a size
     * of 560x560 cells, where every cell is just 1 pixel.
     */
    public CrabWorld()
    {
        super(560, 560, 1);
    }
}
```

Next comes the interesting part:

```
public CrabWorld()
{
    super(560, 560, 1);
}
```

**Concept:**

A **constructor** of
a class is a special
kind of method
that is executed
automatically
whenever a
new instance is
created.

This is called the *constructor* of this class. A constructor looks quite similar to a method, but there are some differences:

■ A constructor has no return type specified between the keyword "public" and the name.

■ The name of a constructor is always the same as the name of the class.

A constructor is a special kind of method that is always automatically executed whenever an instance of this class is created. It can then do what it wants to do to set up this new instance into a starting state.

In our case, the constructor sets the world to the size we want (560 by 560 cells) and a *resolution* (1 pixel per cell). We will discuss world resolution in more detail later in this book.

Since this constructor is executed every time a world is created, we can use it to automatically create our actors. If we insert code into the constructor to create an actor, that code will be executed as well. For example,

```
public CrabWorld()
{
    super(560, 560, 1);
    addObject( new Crab(), 150, 100 );
}
```

This code will automatically create a new crab, and place it at location x=150, y=100 into the world. The location 150,100 is 150 cells from the left edge of the world, and 100 cells from the top. The origin—the 0,0 point—of our coordinate system is at the top left of the world (Figure 4.1).

**Figure 4.1**

The coordinate system of the world

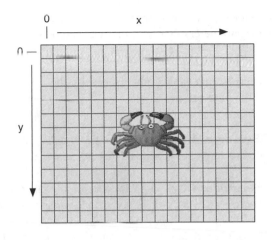

We are using two new things here: the addObject method, and the new statement to create the new crab.

The addObject method is a method of the World class. We can look it up by looking at the class documentation for class World. There, we see that it has the following signature:

```
void addObject(Actor object, int x, int y)
```

Reading the signature from start to finish, this tells us the following:

■ The method does not return a result (void return type).

■ The name of the method is addObject.

■ The method has three parameters, named object, x, and y.

■ The type of the first parameter is Actor, the type of the other two is int.

This method can be used to add a new actor into the world. Since the method belongs to the World class and CrabWorld is a World (it inherits from the World class), this method is available in our CrabWorld class, and we can just call it.

## 4.2 Creating new objects

The addObject method allows us to add an actor object to the world. However, in order to add an object, we must first have an object to add.

The Java keyword new allows us to create new objects of any of the existing classes. For example, the expression

```
new Crab()
```

**Concept:**

Java objects can be created pro-grammatically (from within your code) by using the **new** keyword.

creates a new instance of class Crab. The expression to create new objects always starts with the keyword new, followed by the name of the class we wish to create and a parameter list (which is empty in our example). The parameter list allows us to pass parameters to the constructor. Since we did not specify a constructor for our Crab class, the default parameter list is empty.

When we create a new object, we have to do something with it. We can now use it in place of the actor parameter of the `addObject` method to add this object to the world.

```
addObject( new Crab(), 150, 100);
```

The remaining two parameters specify the *x* and *y* coordinates of the position where we wish to add the object.

---

**Exercise 4.1** Add code to the `CrabWorld` constructor of your own project to create a crab automatically, as discussed above.

**Exercise 4.2** Add code to automatically create three lobsters in the `CrabWorld`. You can choose arbitrary locations for them in the world.

**Exercise 4.3** Add code to create 10 worms at arbitrary locations in the `CrabWorld`.

**Exercise 4.4** Move all the code that creates the objects into a separate method, called `populateWorld`, in the `CrabWorld` class. You need to declare the `populateWorld` method yourself (it takes no parameters and returns nothing) and call it from the constructor. Try it out.

**Exercise 4.5** Use random numbers for the coordinates of the worms. You can do this by replacing your coordinate values with calls to get random numbers from the `Greenfoot` class.

---

You should now have a version of your crab project that places the crab, lobsters, and worms into the world automatically, whenever you compile your scenario. (If you have trouble, look into the *little-crab-5* scenario in the book projects—it includes this code and the remaining changes from this chapter.)

## 4.3 Animating images

The next thing we shall discuss in relation to the crab scenario is animation of the crab image. To make the movement of the crab look a little better, we plan to change the crab so that it moves its legs while it is walking.

Animation is achieved with a simple trick: We have two different images of the crab (in our scenario, they are called *crab.png* and *crab2.png*), and we simply switch the crab's image between these two versions fairly quickly. The position of the crab's legs in these images is slightly different (Figure 4.2).

**Figure 4.2**
Two slightly different images for the crab

a) crab with legs out

b) crab with legs in

The effect of this (switching back and forth between these images) will be that the crab looks as if it is moving its legs.

In order to do this, we have to introduce two new concepts: variables and Greenfoot images.

## 4.4    Greenfoot images

**Concept:**

Greenfoot actors maintain their visible image by holding an object of type GreenfootImage.

Greenfoot provides a class called `GreenfootImage` that helps in using and manipulating images. We can obtain an image by constructing a new `GreenfootImage` object—using Java's new keyword—with the file name of the image file as a parameter to the constructor. For example, to get access to the *crab2.png* image, we can write

```
new GreenfootImage("crab2.png")
```

The file we name here must exist in the scenario's *images* folder.

All Greenfoot actors have images. By default, actors get their image from their class. We assign an image to the class when we create it, and every object created from that class will receive, upon creation, a copy of that same image. That does not mean, however, that all objects of the same class must always keep the same image. Every individual actor can decide to change its image at any time.

> **Exercise 4.6** Check the documentation of the `Actor` class. There are two methods that allow us to change an actor's image. What are they called, and what are their parameters? What do they return?

If you did the exercise above, you will have seen that one method to set an actor's image expects a parameter of type `GreenfootImage`. This is the method we shall use. We can create a `GreenfootImage` object from an image file as described above, and then use the actor's `setImage` method to use it for the actor. Here is a code snippet to do this:

```
setImage(new GreenfootImage("crab2.png"));
```

Note that we do two things in this line: We call the `setImage` method, which expects an image as a parameter:

```
setImage( some-image );
```

And in the place of the image to use, we write

```
new GreenfootImage("crab2.png")
```

This creates the image object from the named image file (*crab2.png*). When the whole line is executed, the inner part of the code—the creation of the `GreenfootImage` object—is executed first. Following that, the `setImage` method call is executed, and the image object we just created is passed as a parameter.

For our purpose, it is better to separate the creation of the image object and the setting of the image. The reason for this is that we want to switch the image back and forth many times while the crab is walking. That means, we want to set the image many times, but we still need to create each of our two images only once.

Thus, we shall first create the images and store them, and later we shall use the stored images (without creating them again) over and over to alternate our displayed image.

To store the two images in our crab object, we need a new construct that we have not used before: a variable.

## 4.5 Instance variables (fields)

Often, our actors need to remember some information. In programming languages, this is achieved by storing the information in a *variable*.

Java supports different kinds of variables. The first one we shall look at here is called an *instance variable*, or *field*. (These two terms are synonymous.) We shall see other kinds of variables later.

An instance variable is a bit of memory that belongs to the object (the *instance* of the class, hence the name). Anything stored in it will be remembered as long as the object exists and can be accessed later.

An instance variable is declared in a class by writing the keyword `private` followed by the type of the variable and the variable name:

> **Concept:**
>
> **Instance variables** (also called **fields**) can be used to store information (objects or values) for later use.

```
private variable-type variable-name;
```

The type of the variable defines what we want to store in it. In our case, since we want to store objects of type `GreenfootImage` in our variable, the type should be `GreenfootImage`. The variable name gives us a chance to give a name to the variable that we can use later to refer to it. It should describe what this variable is used for.

Let us look at our `Crab` class as an example (Code 4.2).

**Code 4.2**

The `Crab` class with two instance variables

```
import greenfoot.*; // (Actor, World, Greenfoot, GreenfootImage)

// comment omitted

public class Crab extends Animal
{
    private GreenfootImage image1;
    private GreenfootImage image2;

    // methods omitted

}
```

In this example, we have declared two variables in our `Crab` class. Both are of type `GreenfootImage`, and they are called `image1` and `image2`.

We will always write instance variable declarations at the top of our class, before the constructors and methods. Java does not enforce this, but it is a good practice so that we can always find variable declarations easily when we need to see them.

> **Exercise 4.7** Before adding this code, right-click a crab object in your world and select Inspect from the crab's popup menu. Make a note of all the variables that are shown in the crab object.
>
> **Exercise 4.8** Why do you think the crab has any variables at all, even though we have not declared any in our `Crab` class?
>
> **Exercise 4.9** Add the variable declarations shown on Code 4.2 above to your version of the `Crab` class. Make sure that the class compiles.
>
> **Exercise 4.10** After adding the variables, inspect your crab object again. Take a note of the variables and their values (shown in the white boxes).

Note that the declaration of these two `GreenfootImage` variables does not give us two `GreenfootImage` objects. It just gives us some empty space to store two objects (Figure 4.3). In this figure, the instance variables are depicted as two white boxes.

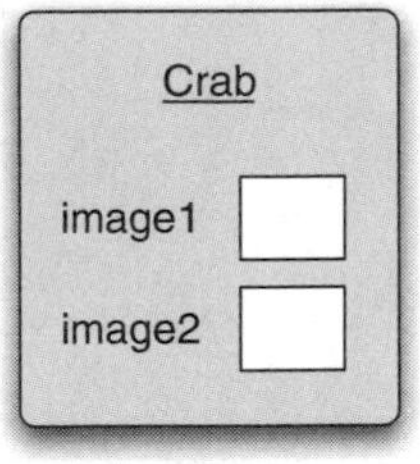

**Figure 4.3**
A crab object with two empty instance variables

```
      Crab

image1  [    ]

image2  [    ]
```

Next, we have to create the two image objects and store them into the variables. The creation of the objects has already been seen above. It was achieved with the code snippet

```
new GreenfootImage("crab2.png")
```

To store the object into the variable, we need a Java construct knows as an *assignment*.

## 4.6 Assignment

An assignment is a statement that enables us to store something into a variable. It is written with an equals symbol:

```
variable = expression;
```

On the left of the equals symbol is the name of the variable we want to store into, on the right is the thing that we want to store. Since the equals symbol stands for assignment, it is also called the *assignment symbol*. We usually read it as "becomes", like this: "variable becomes expression".

In our crab example, we write

```
image1 = new GreenfootImage("crab.png");
image2 = new GreenfootImage("crab2.png");
```

These two lines of code will create the two images we wish to use and store them into our two variables `image1` and `image2`. Following these statements, we have three objects (one crab and two images), and the crab's variables contain references to the images. This is shown in Figure 4.4.

**Figure 4.4**

A crab object with two variables, pointing to image objects

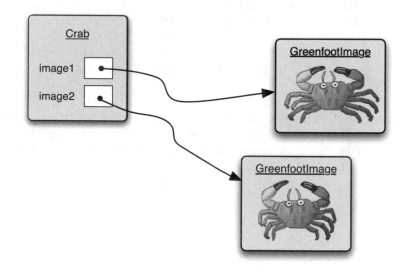

The next question regarding the creation of these images is where to put the code that creates the images and stores them into the variables. Since this should be done only once when the crab object is created, and not every time we act, we cannot put it into the `act` method. Instead, we put this code into a constructor.

## 4.7 Using actor constructors

At the beginning of this chapter, we have seen how to use the constructor of the world class to initialize the world. In a similar manner, we can use a constructor of an actor class to initialize the actor. The code in the constructor is executed once when the actor is created. Code 4.3 shows a constructor for the `Crab` class that initializes the two instance variables by creating images and assigning them to the variables.

**Code 4.3**

Initializing the variables in the constructor

```
import greenfoot.*;  // (Actor, World, Greenfoot, GreenfootImage)

// comment omitted

public class Crab extends Animal
{
    private GreenfootImage image1;
    private GreenfootImage image2;

    /**
     * Create a crab and initialize its two images.
     */
    public Crab()
    {
        image1 = new GreenfootImage("crab.png");
        image2 = new GreenfootImage("crab2.png");
        setImage(image1);
    }

    // methods omitted
}
```

The same rules described for the `World` constructor apply to the `Crab` constructor:

■ The signature of a constructor does not include a return type.

■ The name of the constructor is the same as the name of the class.

■ The constructor is automatically executed when a crab object is created.

The last rule—that the constructor is automatically executed—ensures that the image objects are automatically created and assigned when we create a crab. Thus, after creating the crab, the situation will be as depicted in Figure 4.4.

The last line of the constructor sets the first of the two created images as the crab's current image:

```
setImage(image1);
```

This demonstrates how the name of the variable (`image1`) can be used now to refer to the image object stored in it.

**Exercise 4.11** Add this constructor to your `Crab` class. You will not yet see any change in the behavior of the crab, but the class should compile, and you should be able to create crabs.

> **Exercise 4.12** Inspect your crab object again. Take a note again of the variables and their values. Compare those to the notes you took previously.

## 4.8 Alternating the images

We have now reached a stage where the crab has two images available to do the animation. But we have not done the animation itself yet. This is now relatively simple.

To do the animation, we need to alternate between our two images. In other words, at every step, if we are currently showing image1, we now want to show image2, and *vice versa*. Here is some pseudo-code to express this:

```
if (our current image is image1) then
    use image2 now
else
    use image1 now
```

Pseudo-code, as used here, is a technique expressing a task in a structure that is partly like real Java code, and partly plain English. It often helps in working out how to write our real code. We can now show the same in real Java code (Code 4.4).

**Code 4.4**

Alternating between two images

```
if ( getImage() == image1 )
{
    setImage(image2);
}
else
{
    setImage(image1);
}
```

**Concept:**

We can test whether two things are **equal** by using a double equals symbol: **==**.

In this code segment, we notice several new elements:

- The method getImage can be used to receive the actor's current image.

- The operator = = (two equal signs) can be used to compare one value with another. The result is either *true* or *false*.

- The if statement has an extended form that we have not seen before. This form has an else keyword after the first body of the if statement, followed by another block of statements. We investigate this new form of the if statement in the next section.

> **Pitfall** It is a common mistake to get the assignment operator (=) and the operator to check equality (==) mixed up. If you want to check whether two values or variables are equal, you must write two equal symbols.

## 4.9 The if/else statement

Before moving on, let us investigate the if statement again in some more detail. As we have just seen, an if statement can be written in the form

```
if ( condition )
{
    statements;
}
else
{
    statements;
}
```

This if statement contains two blocks (pairs of curly brackets surrounding a list of statements): the *if clause* and the *else-clause* (in this order).

When this if statement is executed, first the condition is evaluated. If the condition is true, the if-clause is executed, and then execution continues below the else-clause. If the condition is false, the if-clause is not executed, instead we execute the else-clause. Thus, one of the two statement blocks is always executed, but never both.

The else part with the second block is optional—leaving it off leads to the shorter version of the if statement we have seen earlier.

We have now seen everything we need to finalize this task. It is time to get our hands on the keyboard again to try it out.

**Concept:**

The **if/else statement** executes a segment of code when a given condition is true, and a different segment of code when it is false.

**Exercise 4.13** Add the image switching code, as shown in Code 4.4, to the **act** method of your own **Crab** class. Try it out. (If you get an error, fix it. This should work.) Also try clicking the *Act* button instead of the *Run* button in Greenfoot—this allows us to observe the behavior more clearly.

**Exercise 4.14** In Chapter 3, we discussed using separate methods for subtasks, rather than writing more code directly into the **act** method. Do this with the image switching code: Create a new method called **switchImage**, move your image switching code to it, and call this method from within your **act** method.

**Exercise 4.15** Call the **switchImage** method interactively from the crab's popup menu. Does it work?

## 4.10 Counting worms

The final thing we shall discuss with the crabs is counting. We want to add functionality so that the crab counts how many worms it has eaten, and if it has eaten eight worms, we win the game. We also want to play a short "winning sound" when this happens.

To make this happen, we shall need a number of additions to our crab code. We need

- an instance variable to store the current count of worms eaten;
- an assignment that initializes this variable to 0 at the beginning;
- code to increment our count each time we eat a worm; and
- code that checks whether we have eaten eight worms, and stops the game and plays the sound if we have.

Let us do the tasks in this order in which we have listed them here.

We can define a new instance variable by following the pattern introduced in Section 4.5. Below our two existing instance variable definitions, we add the line

```
private int wormsEaten;
```

The word `private` is used at the beginning of all our instance variable definitions. The following two words are the type and the name of our variable. The type `int` indicates that we want to store integers (whole numbers) in this variable, and the name `wormsEaten` indicates what we intend to use it for.

Next, we add the following line to the end of our constructor:

```
wormsEaten = 0;
```

This initializes the `wormsEaten` variable to 0 when the crab is created. Strictly speaking, this is redundant, since instance variables of type `int` are initialized to 0 automatically. However, sometimes we want the initial value to be something other than 0, so writing our own initialization statement is a good practice.

The last bit is to count the worms and check whether we have reached eight. We need to do this every time we eat a worm, so we find our `lookForWorm` method, where we have our code that does the eating of the worms. Here, we add a line of code to increment the worm count:

```
wormsEaten = wormsEaten + 1;
```

In this assignment, the right-hand side of the assignment symbol is evaluated first (`wormsEaten+1`). Thus, we read the current value of `wormsEaten` and add 1 to it. Then we assign the result back to the `wormsEaten` variable. As a result, the variable will be incremented by 1.

Following this, we need an if statement that checks whether we have eaten eight worms yet, and plays the sound and stops execution if we have.

Code 4.5 shows the complete `lookForWorm` method with this code. The sound file used here (*fanfare.wav*) is included in the *sounds* folder in your scenario, so it can just be played.

**Exercise 4.16** Add the code discussed above into your own scenario. Test it, and make sure that it works.

**Code 4.5**

Counting worms
and checking
whether we win

```java
/**
 * Check whether we have stumbled upon a worm.
 * If we have, eat it. If not, do nothing. If we have
 * eaten eight worms, we win.
 */
public void lookForWorm()
{
    if ( canSee(Worm.class) )
    {
        eat(Worm.class);
        Greenfoot.playSound("slurp.wav");

        wormsEaten = wormsEaten + 1;
        if (wormsEaten == 8)
        {
            Greenfoot.playSound("fanfare.wav");
            Greenfoot.stop();
        }
    }
}
```

**Exercise 4.17** As a further test, open an object inspector for your crab object (by selecting Inspect from the crab's popup menu) before you start playing the game Leave the inspector open and keep an eye on the `wormsEaten` variable while you play.

## 4.11 More ideas

The scenario *little-crab-5*, in the book scenarios folder, shows a version of the project that includes all the extensions discussed here.

We will leave this scenario behind now and move on to a different example, although there are many obvious things (and probably many more less obvious things) you can do with this project. Ideas include

- using different images for the background and the actors;
- using more different kinds of actors;
- not moving forward automatically, but only when the up-arrow key is pressed;
- building a two-player game by introducing a second keyboard-controlled class that listens to different keys;
- making new worms pop up when one is eaten (or at random times); and
- many more that you can come up with yourselves.

> **Exercise 4.18** The crab image changes fairly quickly while the crab runs, which makes our crab look a little hyperactive. Maybe it would look nicer if the crab image changed only on every second or third act cycle. Try to implement this. To do this, you could add a counter that gets incremented in the `act` method. Every time it reaches 2 (or 3), the image changes, and the counter is reset to 0.

## 4.12 Summary of programming techniques

In this chapter, we have seen a number of new programming concepts. We have seen how constructors can be used to initialize objects—constructors are always executed when a new object is created. We have seen how to use instance variables—also called *fields*—and assignment statements to store information, and how to access that information later. We have used the new statement to programmatically create new objects, and finally, we have seen the full version of the if statement, which includes an *else* part that is executed when the condition is not true.

With all these techniques together, we can now write quite a good amount of code already.

### Concept summary

- A **constructor** of a class is a special kind of method that is executed automatically whenever a new instance is created.

- Java objects can be created programmatically (from within your code) by using the **new** keyword.

- Greenfoot actors maintain their visible image by holding an object of type **GreenfootImage**. These are stored in an instance variable inherited from class Actor.

- **Instance variables** (also called **fields**) can be used to store information (objects or values) for later use.

- An **assignment statement** assigns an object or a value to a variable.

- When an object is assigned to a variable, the variable contains a **reference** to that object.

- We can test whether two things are **equal** by using a double equals symbol: **==**.

- The **if/else statement** executes a segment of code when a given condition is true, and a different segment of code when it is false.

# Sharing your scenarios

In this section, we will not introduce new programming techniques, but rather go on a quick detour to discuss how you can share what you have created with others. The "others" may be your friend sitting next to you, or another Greenfoot programmer on the other side of the world. In these times of the global Internet this does not make much difference anymore.

## I1.1 Exporting your scenario

When you have finished writing a scenario—maybe a game or a simulation—you may want to enable others to use it. Those users should have the opportunity to start (and restart) the game, but they do not need access to the class diagram or the source code. They should not modify the game, instead they just use it.

In Greenfoot, this is done by exporting the scenario. You can export your scenario by selecting *Export* from the *Scenario* menu. This will show a dialog that lets you choose from three export options: *Application*, *Webpage*, and *Publish*.

## I1.2 Export to application

The first export option is an export to an application. An application is a stand-alone program that users can execute locally on their computer.

To do this, choose *Application* in the export dialog. You can then choose a location and a name for the executable scenario that you are about to create (Figure I1.1).

For a scenario to work well when exported, it is important that it automatically creates all the actors you want to see on the screen at the start of the game. The user will not be able to create objects interactively. This means that usually your world should have a "populate" method, like the one we created for the crab game.

**Concept:**

A **jar file** is a single file with the suffix *jar* that contains all Java classes that belong to an application.

Using this function will create an *executable jar file*. This is a file with a ".*jar*" suffix (short for *Java Archive*), which can be executed on many different operating systems (as long as Java has been installed on that machine). Just double-click the jar file to execute it.

When the application runs, the scenario will look just like it did in Greenfoot, except that the class diagram and the *Compile* button are not present. The user can run the scenario, but not edit or compile.

**Figure I1.1**
Exporting a scenario
to an application

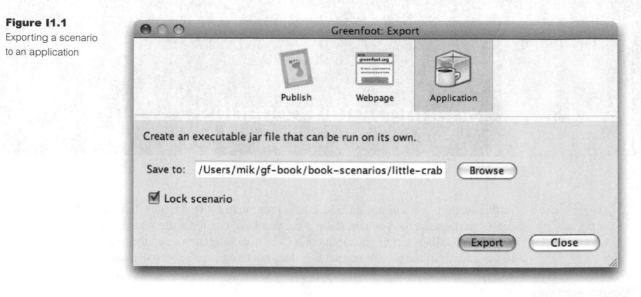

The "Lock scenario" option disables the moving of actors in the world before starting the application, as well as removing the *Act* button and the execution speed slider. If you have a game, you typically want to lock the scenario, whereas for a simulation or other more experimental scenarios you may want to leave it unlocked to allow users to experiment more.

## I1.3  Export to a web page

The second option is to export your scenario to a web page (Figure I1.2). The options in the export dialog are as before, but this function creates a web page (in HTML format) and converts your scenario to an applet that will run in that web page.

You can execute your scenario by opening the generated web page in a web browser.

**Figure I1.2**
Export to a web
page

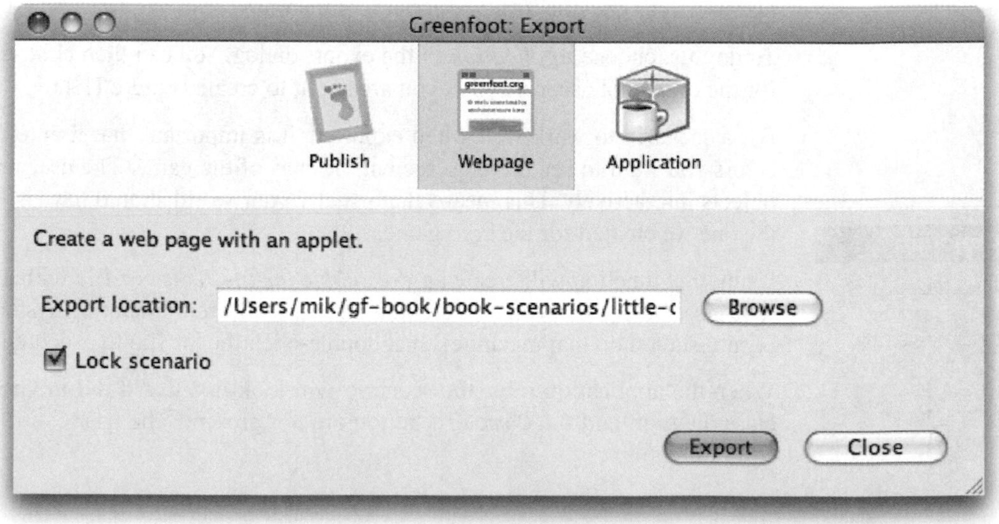

If you have access to a web server, you can now publish this page on the web. If you do not have access to a web server, then the next option may be for you.

## I1.4  Publishing on the Greenfoot Gallery

The last export option you have is to publish your scenario to the *Greenfoot Gallery*. The Greenfoot Gallery is a public web site (at the address http://greenfootgallery.org) that allows Greenfoot users to upload their Greenfoot scenarios for the world to see and play.

The export dialog (Figure I1.3) shows the site address at the top. Click here to open the web site and see what is there. It is probably best if you have a look through the site first.

**Figure I1.3**
Publish to the
Greenfoot Gallery

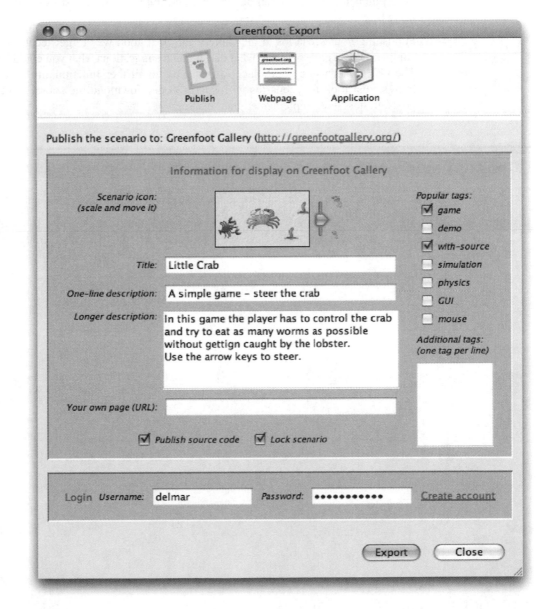

**Concept:**

An **applet** is a version of a Java program that can run on a web page inside a web browser.

In the Gallery, everyone can view and execute scenarios, but if you want to rate them, leave comments, or upload your own scenarios, you need to create an account on the site. This is quick and easy.

After creating an account, you can easily upload your own scenario to the Greenfoot Gallery, using the dialog shown in Figure I1.3. The dialog allows you to add an icon, a description, and tags that identify your scenario.

If you choose to publish the source code (using the `Publish source code` checkbox), your full source code will be copied to the Gallery site, where everybody else can then download it, read it, and make their own versions of your scenario.

Your published scenarios can be changed and improved later just by exporting again with the same title.

Publishing your scenarios to the Gallery can be a good way to get feedback from other users: comments on what works and what doesn't, and suggestions what you could add to the program. The Gallery is also a good place to get ideas for further functionality, or to learn how to do things. Just look for scenarios with source code, download the source, and check how other programmers have implemented their classes.

## Concept summary

- A **jar file** is a single file with the suffix *jar* that contains all Java classes that belong to an application.

- An **applet** is a version of a Java program that can run on a web page inside a web browser.

# Making music.
# An on-screen piano

| | |
|---|---|
| **topics:** | sound |
| **concepts:** | abstraction, loops, arrays, OO structure |

In this chapter we shall start on a new scenario: a piano that we can play with our computer keyboard. Figure 5.1 shows what it could look like once we're finished.

We start again with opening a scenario from the book scenarios: *piano-1*. This is a version of our scenario that has the resources in it that we will need (the images and the sound files), but not much else. We shall use this as the base scenario to start writing the code to build the piano.

**Figure 5.1**
The goal for this chapter: an on-screen piano

**Exercise 5.1** Open the scenario *piano-1* and examine the code for the two existing classes, **Piano** and **Key**. Make sure you know what code is present and what it does.

> **Exercise 5.2** Create an object of class **Key** and place it into the world. Create several of them and place them next to each other.

## 5.1 Animating the key

When you examine the existing code, you see that not much is there at present: The `Piano` class only specifies the size and resolution of the world, and the `Key` class contains only method stubs (empty methods) for the constructor and the `act` method (shown in Code 5.1).

**Code 5.1**

The initial **Key** class

```
import greenfoot.*; // (World, Actor, GreenfootImage, and Greenfoot)

public class Key extends Actor
{
    /**
     * Create a new key.
     */
    public Key()
    {
    }

    /**
     * Do the action for this key.
     */
    public void act()
    {
    }
}
```

We can start experimenting by creating an object of class `Key` and placing it into the world. You see that its image is that of a simple white key, and it does nothing at all when we run the scenario.

Our first task will be to animate the piano key: When we press a key on the keyboard, we would like the piano key on screen to change so that it appears to be pressed down. The scenario as it is already contains two image files named *white-key.png* and *white-key-down.png*, which we can use to show these two states. (It also contains two more image files, *black-key.png* and *black-key-down.png*, which we shall use later for the black keys.) The *white-key.png* image is the one that we currently see when we create a key.

We can create the effect of the key being pressed quite easily by switching between the two images when a specific key on the keyboard is pressed. Code 5.2 shows a first attempt at this.

**Code 5.2**

First version of
the act method:
changing images

```
public void act()
{
    if ( Greenfoot.isKeyDown("g") ) {
        setImage ("white-key-down.png");
    }
    else {
        setImage ("white-key.png");
    }
}
```

In this code, we have chosen an arbitrary key on the computer keyboard (the "g" key) to react to. Which key we use at this stage does not really matter—eventually we want to attach different piano keys to several of our keyboard keys. When the key is pressed on the keyboard, we show the "down" image; when it is not being pressed, we show the "up" image.

> **Exercise 5.3** Implement this version of the act method in your own scenario. Test it—make sure it works.

While this version works, it has a problem: The image is set not only once when it changes, but continuously. Every time the act method executes, the image is set to either one of the two images, even though it might already show the correct image. For example, if the "g" key is not being pressed, the image will be set to *white-key.png*, even if this was already the displayed image.

This problem does not seem too serious at first. After all, setting the image when it is not needed is merely unnecessary, but not incorrect. There are several reasons why we want to fix this, though. One reason is that it is good practice to not waste processor resources by doing unnecessary work. Another reason is that we will add sound for the key soon, and then it does matter. When we press a key, it makes a big difference whether the key's sound is heard once, or over and over again.

So, let us improve our code by ensuring that the image is only set when it actually changes. To do this, we add a boolean field to our class to remember whether the key is currently down or not. We call this field isDown, and its declaration looks as follows:

```
private boolean isDown;
```

We will store true in this field while the piano key is down, and false while it isn't.

We can then check whether our keyboard key has just now been pressed: If our isDown field is false, but the "g" key on the keyboard is being pressed, it must have been pressed just a moment ago. Conversely, if our isDown field is true (we think the key is down), but the "g" key on the keyboard is not down, then it must have been released just now. In these two situations, we can then change the image. Code 5.3 shows the complete act method implementing this idea.

**Code 5.3**

Only set the image when it needs to change

```java
public void act()
{
    if ( !isDown && Greenfoot.isKeyDown("g") ) {
        setImage ("white-key-down.png");
        isDown = true;
    }
    if ( isDown && !Greenfoot.isKeyDown("g") ) {
        setImage ("white-key.png");
        isDown = false;
    }
}
```

In both cases, we make sure to set the `isDown` field to the new state if we detect a change.

This code makes use of two new symbols: the exclamation mark (`!`) and the double ampersand (`&&`).

Both are logical operators. The exclamation mark means *NOT*, while the double ampersand means *AND*.

**Concept:**

**Logic operators**, such as **&&** (AND) and **!** (NOT), can be used to combine multiple boolean expressions into one boolean expression.

Thus, the following lines from the `act` method

```java
if ( !isDown && Greenfoot.isKeyDown("g") ) {
    setImage ("white-key-down.png");
    isDown = true;
}
```

can be read a little more informally (attention: not Java code!) as

```java
if ( (not isDown) and Greenfoot.isKeyDown("g") ) ...
```

The same code, even more informally, can be read as

```java
if ( the-piano-key-is-not-currently-down and the-keyboard-key-is-down) {
    change the image to show the "down" image;
    remember that the piano key is down now;
}
```

Have a look at Code 5.3 again, and make sure you understand the code shown there.

A full list of all available logic operators is given in Appendix D.

**Exercise 5.4** Implement the new version of the `act` method in your own scenario. It will not appear to do anything different than before, but it is a necessary preparation for what we shall do next. Don't forget that you also have to add the **boolean isDown** field at the beginning of your class.

## 5.2  Producing the sound

The next thing we shall do is to ensure that pressing the key makes a sound. To do this, we add a new method to the Key class, called play. We can add this method in the editor, below the act method. For a start, we can write the comment, signature, and an empty body for the new method:

```
/**
 * Play the note of this key.
 */
public void play()
{

}
```

While this code does not do anything (the method body is empty), it should compile.

The implementation for this method is quite simple: We just want to play a single sound file. The *piano-1* scenario, which you used to start this project, has a collection of sound files included (in the *sounds* subfolder), each of which contains the sound of a single piano key. The names of the sound files are *2a.wav*, *2b.wav*, *2c.wav*, *2c#.wav*, *2d.wav*, *2d#.wav*, *2e.wav*, and so on. Of these, let us just pick a more or less random note—say *3a.wav*, a middle *a*—to play for our test key.

To actually play this note, we can use the playSound method from the Greenfoot class again:

```
Greenfoot.playSound("3a.wav");
```

This is the only code needed in the play method. The complete method implementation is shown in Code 5.4.

**Code 5.4**

Playing the note for the key

```
/**
 * Play the note of this key.
 */
public void play()
{
    Greenfoot.playSound("3a.wav");
}
```

**Exercise 5.5** Implement the play method in your own version of the scenario. Make sure that the code compiles.

**Exercise 5.6** Test your method. You can do this by creating an object of class **Key**, right-clicking the object and invoking the play method from the object's popup menu.

We are almost there now. We can produce the key's sound by interactively invoking the play method, and we can run the scenario and press a keyboard key ("g") to create the appearance of the piano key being pressed.

All we need to do now is to play the sound when the keyboard key is pressed.

To play the sound programmatically (from your code), we can just call our own `play` method, like this:

```
play();
```

**Exercise 5.7** Add code to your Key class so that the key's note is played when the associated keyboard key is pressed. To do this, you need to figure out where the call to the `play` method should be added. Test.

**Exercise 5.8** What happens when you create two keys, run the scenario and press the "g" key? Do you have any ideas what we need to do to make them react to different keyboard keys?

All the changes described this far are available in the book scenarios as *piano-2*. If you had problems that you could not solve, or if you just want to compare your solution with ours, have a look at this version.

## 5.3 Abstraction: Creating multiple keys

We have reached a stage where we can create a piano key that reacts to one key of our computer keyboard and plays a single piano note. The problem now is obvious: When we create multiple keys, they all react to the same keyboard key, and all produce the same note. We need to change that.

The current limitation comes from the fact that we *hard-coded* the keyboard key name ("g") and the sound file name ("3a.wav") into our class. That means, we used these names directly, without a chance to change them short of changing the source code and recompiling.

When writing computer programs, writing code that can solve one very specific task—such as finding the square root of 1,764 or playing a middle-*a* piano key sound—is well and good, but not incredibly useful. Generally, we would like to write code that can solve a whole *class* of problem (such as finding the square root of any number, or playing a whole range of piano key sounds). If we do this, our program becomes much more useful.

To achieve this, we use a technique called *abstraction*. Abstraction occurs in computing in many different forms and contexts—this is one of them.

**Concept:**

**Abstraction** occurs in many different forms in programming. One of them is the technique to write code that can solve a whole class of problems, rather than a single specific problem.

We shall use abstraction to turn our Key class from a class that can create objects that play a middle-*a* when the "g" key is pressed on the keyboard into one that can create objects that can play a range of notes when different keyboard keys are pressed.

The main idea to achieving this is to use a variable for the name of the keyboard key we react to, and another variable for the name of the sound file we then want to play.

**Code 5.5**

Generalizing for
multiple keys: making
the key and note
variable

```java
public class Key extends Actor
{
    private boolean isDown;
    private String key;
    private String sound;

    /**
     * Create a new key linked to a given keyboard key, and
     * with a given sound.
     */
    public Key(String keyName, String soundFile)
    {
        key = keyName;
        sound = soundFile;
    }

    // methods omitted.
}
```

Code 5.5 shows the start of a solution to this. Here, we use two additional fields—`key` and `sound`—to store the name of the key and the sound file we want to use. We also add two parameters to the constructor, so that these bits of information can be passed in when the key object is being created, and we make sure that we store these parameter values into the fields in the constructor body.

We have now made an abstraction of our `Key` class. Now, when we create a new `Key` object, we can specify which keyboard key it should react to, and which sound file it should play. Of course, we haven't written the code yet that actually uses these variables—that remains to be done.

We will leave this as an exercise for you.

**Exercise 5.9** Implement the changes discussed above. That is, add fields for the key and the sound file, and add a constructor with two parameters that initializes those fields.

**Exercise 5.10** Modify your code so that your key object reacts to the key and plays the sound file specified on construction. Test! (Construct multiple keys with different sounds.)

We have now reached a point where we can create a set of keys to play a range of notes. (Currently, we have only white keys, but we can already build half a piano with this.) This version of the project is in the book scenarios as *piano-3*.

Constructing all the keys, however, is a bit tedious. Currently, we have to create every piano key by hand, typing in all the parameters. What's worse: every time we make a change to the source code, we have to start all over again. It is time to write some code to create the keys for us.

## 5.4 Building the piano

We would now like to write some code in the `Piano` class that creates and places the piano keys for us. Adding a single key (or a few keys) is quite straight forward: By adding the following line to the `Piano`'s constructor, a key is created and placed into the world each time we re-initialize the scenario:

```
addObject (new Key ("g", "3a.wav"), 300, 180);
```

Remember that the expression

```
new Key ("g", "3a.wav")
```

creates a new key object (with a specified key and sound file), while the statement

```
addObject ( some-object, 300, 180);
```

inserts the given object into the world at the specified *x* and *y* coordinates. The exact coordinates 300 and 180 are picked somewhat arbitrarily at this stage.

> **Exercise 5.11** Add code to your `Piano` class so that it automatically creates a piano key and places in into the world.
>
> **Exercise 5.12** Change the *y*-coordinate at which the key is placed, so that the piano key appears exactly at the top of the piano (i.e., the top of the piano key should line up with the top of the piano itself). Hint: The key image is 280 pixels high and 63 pixels wide.
>
> **Exercise 5.13** Write code to create a second piano key that plays a middle-*g* (sound file name *3g.wav*) when the "f" key is pressed on the keyboard. Place this key exactly to the left of the first key (without any gap or overlap).

Earlier in this book, we have discussed the value of using separate methods for separate tasks. Creating all the keys is a logically distinct task, so let us place the code for it into a separate method. It will do exactly the same thing, but the code is clearer to read.

> **Exercise 5.14** In the `Piano` class, create a new method named `makeKeys()`. Move your code that creates your keys into this method. Call this method from the Piano's constructor. Make sure to write a comment for your new method.

We could now go ahead and insert a whole list of `addObject` statements to create all the keys we need for our keyboard. That is, however, not the best way of achieving what we want to do.

# Using loops: The while loop

Programming languages offer you a specific construct to do a similar task repeatedly: a *loop*.

A loop is a programming language construct that allows us to express commands such as *"Do this statement 20 times"* or *"Call these two methods 3 million times"* easily and concisely (without writing 3 million lines of code). Java has several different kinds of loop. The one we shall investigate now is called a *while loop*.

A `while` loop has the following form:

```
while ( condition )
{
    statement;
    statement;
    ...
}
```

**Concept:**

A **loop** is a statement in programming languages that can execute a section of code multiple times.

The Java keyword `while` is followed by a condition in parentheses and a block (a pair of curly brackets) containing one or more statements. These statements will be executed over and over, as long is the condition is `true`.

A very common pattern is a loop that executes some statements a given number of times. To do this, we use a *loop variable* as a counter. It is common practice to name a loop variable i, so we shall do this as well. Here is an example that executes the body of the while loop 100 times:

```
int i = 0;
while (i < 100)
{
    statement;
    statement;
    ...
    i = i + 1;
}
```

**Concept:**

A **local variable** is a variable that is declared inside a method body. It is used for temporary storage.

There are several things worth noting in this code. First, it uses a concept that we have not encountered before: a *local variable*.

A local variable is a variable similar to a field. We can use it to store values in it, such as an integer number, or object references.

It differs from fields in several respects:

- A local variable is declared inside a method body, not at the beginning of the class;

- It has no visibility modifier (private or public) in front of it; and

- It exists only until the current method finishes running, then it will be erased.[1]

---

[1] Strictly speaking, this is not exactly correct. Local variables can also be declared inside other blocks, such as inside if statements or the body of a loop. They exist only until execution exits the block they were declared in. The statement above is, however, correct if the local variable was declared at the beginning of a method.

A local variable is declared by just writing the type of a variable, followed by its name:

```
int i;
```

After declaring the variable, we can assign a value. Here are these two statements together:

```
int i;
i = 0;
```

Java allows a shortcut to write these two statements in one line, declaring the variable and assigning a value:

```
int i = 0;
```

This line has exactly the same effect as the two-line version. This is the variant we have used in the code pattern for the while loop above.

Look at the pattern for the loop again—we should now be able to roughly understand what it does. We use a variable i and initialize it to 0. Then we repeatedly execute the body of the while loop, counting up i every time we do so. We continue this as long as i is less than 100. When we reach 100, we stop the loop. Execution will then continue with the code following the loop body.

There are two further details worth pointing out:

■ We use the statement i = i + 1; at the end of the loop body to increment our loop variable by 1 every time we have executed the loop. This is important. It is a common error to forget to increment the loop counter. The variable would then never change, the condition would always remain true, and the loop would continue looping forever. This is called an *infinite loop*, and is the cause of many errors in programs.

■ Our condition says that we execute the loop while i is less than (<) 100, not less than or equal (<=). So the loop will not be executed when i is equal to 100. At first glance, one might think that this means that the loop executes only 99 times, not 100 times. But this is not so. Because we started counting at 0, not at 1, we do execute 100 times (counting from 0 to 99). It is very common to start counting from 0 in computer programs—we will see some advantages of doing so soon.

Now that we know about a while loop, we can use this construct to create all our piano keys.

Our piano will have 12 white keys. We can now create 12 keys by placing our statement to create a key inside the body of a loop that executes 12 times:

```
int i = 0;
while (i < 12)
{
    addObject (new Key ("g", "3a.wav"), 300, 140);
    i = i + 1;
}
```

**Exercise 5.15** Replace the code in your own **makeKeys** method with the loop shown here. Try it out. What do you observe?

Trying out this code, it first looks as if only one key was created. This is deceptive, however. We do indeed get 12 keys, but since they have all been inserted at exactly the same coordinates, they are all lying right on top of each other, and we cannot see them very well. Try moving the keys in the piano world with your mouse pointer and you will see that they are all there.

**Exercise 5.16** How can you change your code so that the keys do not all appear at exactly the same place? Can you change your code so that they get placed exactly next to each other?

The reason the keys all appeared on top of each other is that we inserted them all at the fixed location 300,140 into the world. We now want to insert every key at a different location. This is now actually quite easy to do: We can make use of our loop variable i to achieve this.

**Exercise 5.17** How many times does our loop body execute? What are the values of i during each of the executions?

We can now replace the fixed $x$-coordinate 300 with an expression that includes the variable i:

```
addObject (new Key (“g”, “3a.wav”), i*63, 140);
```

(The asterisk "*" is the operator for multiplication. Appendix D lists other operators that you can use with integer numbers.)

We have chosen i*63, because we know that the image of each key is 63 pixels wide. The values for i, as the loop executes, are 0, 1, 2, 3, and so on. So the keys will be placed at $x$-coordinates 0, 63, 126, 189, and so on.

When we try this we notice that the left-most key is not placed very well. Since object placement in Greenfoot refers to the center point of an object, the center of the first key is placed at $x$-coordinate 0, which places the key half out of the screen. To fix this, we just add a fixed offset to each key coordinate. The offset is chosen so that the keys as a whole appear in the middle of our piano:

```
addObject (new Key (“g”, “3a.wav”), i*63 + 54, 140);
```

The $y$-coordinate can remain constant, since we want all keys at the same height.

**Exercise 5.18** Challenge exercise. (Do this exercise only if you are fairly confident about your programming. If you are just beginning, you may like to skip this exercise.)

Using fixed numbers in your code, such as the 140 or 63 in the statement above, is usually not the best solution, since it makes your code vulnerable to breaking when things change. For example, if we replace the key images with nicer images that have a different size, our code would not place them correctly.

> We can avoid using those numbers directly by calling the `getWidth()` and `getHeight()` methods of the key's image. To do this, first assign the key object to a local variable of type `Key` when you create it, and then use `key.getImage().getWidth()` in place of the 63. Do a similar thing with the height.
>
> Replacing the 54 requires you to also use the `getWidth()` method of the piano's image.
>
> After doing this, our code will always place the keys nicely, even if their size changes.

Our code now places our white keys nicely—that's a good step forward. The most obvious problem now is that all piano keys react to the same keyboard key and play the same note. Fixing this again requires a new programming construct: an *array*.

## 5.6 Using arrays

Currently, our 12 keys are created, and placed at appropriate locations on the screen, but they all react to the "g" key, and they all play the same note. This is despite the fact that we have prepared our keys to accept different keyboard keys and sound files in the constructor. However, since all our keys are created by the same line of source code (executed in a loop), they are all created with "g" and "3a.wav" as parameters.

The solution is similar to the change we made in regards to the *x*-coordinate: We should use variables for the keyboard key and the sound file name, and assign different values to them each time the loop executes.

This is more problematic than in the case with the *x*-coordinate, though. The correct keys and sound file names cannot be computed as easily. So where do we get the values from?

Our answer is: We will store them in an array.

An array is an object that can hold many variables, and thus can store many values. We can show this in a diagram. Assume we have a variable named "name" of type `String`. To this variable, we assign the `String` "Fred":

```
String name;
name = "Fred";
```

Figure 5.2 illustrates this example.

This case is very simple. The variable is a container that can hold a value. The value is stored in the variable.

In case of an array, we get a separate object—the array object—that holds many variables. We can then store a reference to that array object in our own variable (Figure 5.3).

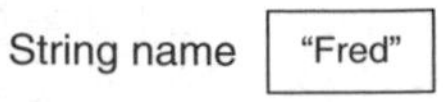

**Figure 5.2**
A simple `String` variable

String name    "Fred"

**Figure 5.3**
An array of Strings

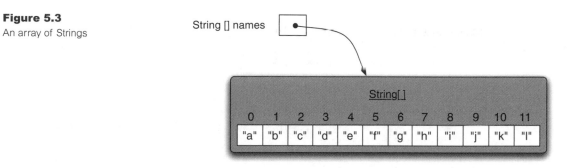

The Java code to create this situation is as follows:

```
String[] names;
names = { "a","b","c","d","e","f","g","h","i","j","k","l" };
```

In the variable declaration, the pair of square brackets ([ ]) indicates that the type of the variable is an array. The word before the brackets indicates the *element type* of the array, that is, the type that each entry in the array should have. Thus String[ ] denotes an array of Strings, while int[ ] denotes an array of integers.

The expression

```
{ "a","b","c","d","e","f","g","h","i","j","k","l" }
```

creates the array object and fills it with the Strings "a" to "l". This array object is then assigned to our variable names. We can see from the diagram that, when an array object is assigned to a variable, the variable then contains a pointer to that object.

Once we have our array variable in place, we can access individual elements in the array by using an *index*—a position number in the array object. In Figure 5.3, the index of each individual String is shown above each array element. Note that counting again starts at 0, so the String "a" is at position 0, "b" is at position 1, and so on.

In Java, we access array elements by attaching the index in square brackets to the array name. For example,

```
names[3]
```

**Concept:**

Individual **elements** in an array are accessed using square brackets ([ ]) and an index to specify the array element.

accesses the element in the names array at index 3—the String "d".

For our piano project, we can now prepare two arrays: one with the names of the keyboard keys (in order) for our piano keys, and one with the names of the sound files for those piano keys. We can declare fields in the Piano class for those arrays and store the filled arrays. Code 5.6 illustrates this.

Note that the values in the whiteKeys array are the keys on the middle row of my computer keyboard. Keyboards are slightly different on different systems and in different countries, so you may have to change these to match your own keyboard. The other slightly odd thing here is the String "\\". The backslash character (\) is called an *escape character* and has a special meaning in Java Strings. To create a String that contains the backslash as a normal character, you have to type it twice. So typing the String "\\" in your Java source code actually creates the String "\".

**Code 5.6**

Creating arrays for
keys and notes

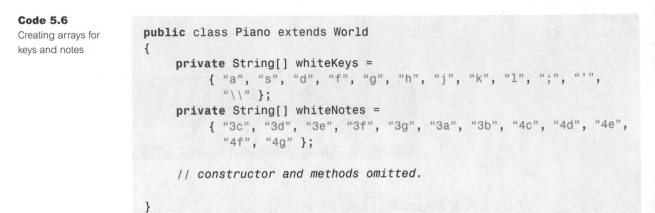

```java
public class Piano extends World
{
    private String[] whiteKeys =
        { "a", "s", "d", "f", "g", "h", "j", "k", "l", ";", "'",
          "\\" };
    private String[] whiteNotes =
        { "3c", "3d", "3e", "3f", "3g", "3a", "3b", "4c", "4d", "4e",
          "4f", "4g" };

    // constructor and methods omitted.

}
```

Now we have arrays available listing the keys and sound file names that we want to use for our piano keys. We can now adapt our loop in the makeKeys method to make use of the array elements to create appropriate keys. Code 5.7 shows the resulting source code.

**Code 5.7**

Creating piano keys
with keyboard keys
and notes from
arrays

```java
/**
 * Create the piano keys and place them in the world.
 */
private void makeKeys()
{
    int i = 0;
    while (i < whiteKeys.length)
    {
        Key key = new Key(whiteKeys[i], whiteNotes[i] + ".wav");
        addObject(key, 54 + (i*63), 140);
        i = i + 1;
    }
}
```

A number of things are worth noting:

■ We have moved the creation of the new key out of the addObject method call into a separate line, and assigned the key object initially to a local variable, called key. This was just done for clarity: The line got very long and busy, and it was quite hard to read. Splitting it into two steps makes it easier to read.

■ The parameters for the Key constructor access whiteKeys[i] and whiteNotes[i]. That is, we use our loop variable i as the array index to access all the different key strings and note file names in turn.

■ We use a plus symbol (+) with whiteKeys[i] and a String (".wav"). The variable whiteKeys[i] is also a String, so the plus symbol is used with two String operands. When

**Concept:**

The plus symbol (+), when used with Strings, stands for **String concatenation**. It merges two Strings together into one.

+ is used with Strings, it performs *string concatenation*. String concatenation is an operation that sticks two Strings together and turns them into a single String. In other words, here, we append the String ".wav" to the `whiteNotes[i]` value. This is because the name stored in the array is of the form "3c", while the file name on disk is "3c.wav". We could have stored the full file name in the array, but since the suffix is the same for all notes files, this seemed unnecessary. Just adding it here saves us some typing.

■ We have also replaced the 12 in the condition of the `while` loop with `whiteKeys.length`. The `.length` attribute of an array will return the number of elements in this array. In our case, we do have 12 elements, so leaving the 12 in place would have worked. However, using the length attribute is safer. Should we one day decide to use more or fewer keys, our loop will still do the right thing, without the need to change the condition.

With these changes, our piano should now be playable with the middle row of keys on our keyboard, and it should produce different notes for different keys.

**Exercise 5.19** Make the changes discussed above in your own scenario. Make sure that all keys work. If your keyboard layout is different, adapt the `whiteKeys` array to match your keyboard.

**Exercise 5.20** The *sounds* folder of the piano scenario contains more notes than the ones we are using here. Change the piano so that the keys are one octave lower than they are now. That is, use the sound "2c" instead of "3c" for the first key, and move up from there.

**Exercise 5.21** If you like, you can make your keys produce entirely different sounds. You can record you own sounds using sound recording software, or you can find sound files on the Internet. Move the sound files into the *sounds* folder, and make your keys play them.

The version we have now is in the book scenarios as *piano-4*.

The missing part now is quite obvious: We have to add the black keys.

There is nothing really new in this. We essentially have to do very similar things again as we did for the white keys. We will leave this as an exercise for you to do. However, doing it all in one chunk is quite a substantial job. In general, when approaching a larger task, it is a good idea to break it down into several smaller steps. Thus, we will break this task down into a sequence of exercises that approaches the solution one step at a time.

**Exercise 5.22** Currently, our **Key** class can only produce white keys. This is because we have hard-coded the file names of the key images ("white-key.png" and "white-key-down.png"). Use abstraction to modify the **Key** class so that it can show either white or black keys. This is similar to what we did with the key name and sound file name: Introduce two fields and two parameters for the two image file names, and then use the variables instead of the hard-coded file names. Test by creating some black and some white keys.

**Exercise 5.23** Modify your `Piano` class so that it adds two black keys at an arbitrary location.

**Exercise 5.24** Add two more arrays to the `Piano` class for the keyboard keys and notes of the black keys.

**Exercise 5.25** Add another loop in the `makeKeys` method in the `Piano` class that creates and places the black keys. This is made quite tricky by the fact that black keys are not as evenly spaced as white keys—they have gaps (see Figure 5.1). Can you come up with a solution to this? Tip: Create a special entry in your array where the gaps are, and use that to recognize the gaps. (Read the note below these exercises first before you start. This is a hard task! You may want to look at the solution in *piano-5* if you cannot figure it out.)

**Exercise 5.26** The full implementation of this project, *piano-5*, also includes another short method to show a line of text on the screen. Study it, and make some changes: Change the wording of the text; change its color; and move the text so that it is horizontally centered.

**Concept:**

The type **String** is defined by a normal class. It has many useful methods, which we can look up in the Java library documentation.

### Note: The String class

The type `String` that we have used many times before is defined by a class. Find this class in the Java library documentation and have a look at its methods. There are many, and some of them are often very useful.

You will see methods to create substrings, to find out the length of a string, to convert the case, and much more.

Especially interesting for Exercise 5.25 above may be the `equals` method that allows you to compare the string with another string. It will return `true` if the two strings are the same.

This is as far as we go with this project. The piano is more or less complete now. We can play simple tunes, and we can even play chords (multiple keys at the same time).

Feel free to extend this if you like. How about adding a second set of sounds, and then adding a switch on screen that allows you to switch from the piano sounds to your alternate sounds?

## 5.7 Summary of programming techniques

In this chapter, we have seen two very fundamental and important concepts for more sophisticated programming: loops and arrays. Loops allow us to write code that executes a sequence of statements many times over. The loop construct we have discussed is called a *while loop*. Java has other loops as well, which we will encounter shortly. We will use loops in many of our programs, so it is essential to understand them.

Within the loop, we often use the loop counter to perform calculations or to generate different values in every loop iteration.

The other major new concept we used was an array. An array can provide many variables (all of the same type) in one single object. Often, loops are used to process an array if we need to do something to each of its elements. Elements are accessed using square brackets.

Another very fundamental technique we encountered was abstraction. In this case, it appeared through the use of constructor parameters to create code that could handle a whole class of problems instead of a single specific problem.

We have also encountered a few new operators: We have seen the AND and NOT operators for boolean expressions (&& and !), and we have seen that the plus operator (+) performs string concatenation when applied to Strings. The `String` class is documented in the Java API documentation and has many useful methods.

## Concept summary

- **Logic operators**, such as && (AND) and ! (NOT), can be used to combine multiple boolean expressions into one boolean expression.

- **Abstraction** occurs in many different forms in programming. One of them is the technique to write code that can solve a whole class of problems, rather than a single specific problem.

- A **loop** is a statement in programming languages that can execute a section of code multiple times.

- A **local variable** is a variable that is declared inside a method body. It is used for temporary storage.

- An **array** is an object that holds multiple variables. These can be accessed using an **index**.

- Individual **elements** in an array are accessed using square brackets ( [ ] ) and an index to specify the array element.

- The plus symbol (+), when used with Strings, stands for **String concatenation**. It merges two Strings together into one.

- The type **String** is defined by a normal class. It has many useful methods, which we can look up in the Java library documentation.

# Interacting objects:
# Newton's Lab

| topics: | objects interacting with each other, using helper classes, using classes from the Java library |
|---|---|
| concepts: | collection, list, for-each loop, standard class library |

In this chapter, we shall investigate more sophisticated interactions between objects in a world. As a start, we shall investigate one of the most universal interactions between objects anywhere: Gravity.

In this scenario, we are dealing with celestial bodies (such as stars and planets). We shall simulate the motion of these bodies through space, using Newton's law of universal gravitation. (We now know that Newton's formulas are not quite accurate, and that Einstein's theory of general relativity describes the motions of planets more precisely, but Newton is still good enough for our simple simulation. Both are shown in Figure 6.1.)

If you are a little worried about dealing with physics and formulas, don't worry. We do not need to go very deep into it, and the formula we shall use is really quite simple. At the end, we shall turn this scenario into an artistic experiment with sound and visual effects. If you are more

**Figure 6.1**

Isaac Newton and
Albert Einstein.

Newton: Portrait by Godfrey Kneller, 1689. Einstein: Portrait by Ferdinand Schmutzer, 1921

technically interested, you can work more on the physics. If your interest is more artistic, you can concentrate on this aspect instead.

 ## 6.1 The starting point: Newton's Lab

We shall start this project by investigating a partly implemented version of this scenario. Open the *Newtons-Lab-1* scenario from the *book-scenarios* folder. You will see that a world subclass already exists (called `Space`). We also have classes `SmoothMover`, `Body`, and `Vector` (Figure 6.2).

> **Exercise 6.1** Open the *Newtons-Lab-1* scenario. Try it out (i.e., place some bodies into space). What do you observe?

**Figure 6.2**
The Newton's Lab scenario

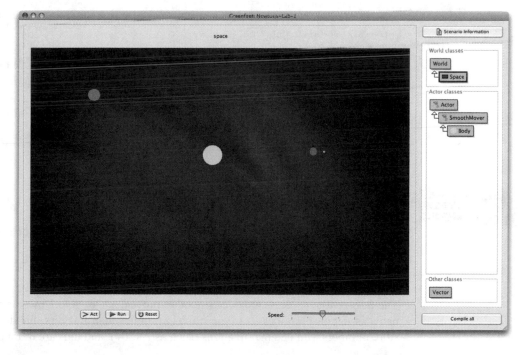

When you try to run this scenario, you will notice that you can place objects (of type `Body`) into space, but these bodies do not move, and they do not act in any interesting way yet.

Before we get into extending the implementation, let us investigate the scenario a little more closely.

By right-clicking on the title of the world (the word "space" near the top), we can see and invoke the public methods of the `Space` class (Figure 6.3).

**Figure 6.3**
The `World` methods
in Newton's Lab

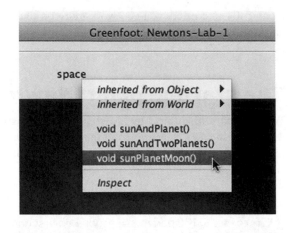

---

**Exercise 6.2** Invoke the different public methods of the **Space** object. What do they do?

**Exercise 6.3** When you have a star or planet in your world, right-click it to see what public methods it has. What are they?

**Exercise 6.4** Invoke the `sunPlanetMoon` method from the public methods of **Space**. Find out and write down the mass of the Sun, the planet, and the Moon.

**Exercise 6.5** Have a look at the source code of the **Space** class and see how the public methods here are implemented.

---

## 6.2 Helper classes: SmoothMover and Vector

In this scenario, we are using two general purpose helper classes: `SmoothMover` and `Vector`. These are classes that add functionality to a given scenario, and can be used in different scenarios for similar purposes. (These two classes are in fact used in a number of different existing projects.)

The `SmoothMover` class provides smoother movement for actors by storing the actor's coordinates as decimal numbers (of type `double`), rather than integers. Fields of type `double` can store numbers with decimal fractions (such as 2.4567), and thus are more precise than integers.

For displaying the actor on screen, the coordinates will still be rounded to integers, since the location for painting on screen must always be a whole pixel. Internally, however, the location is held as a decimal number.

A `SmoothMover` can, for example, have the *x*-coordinate 12.3. If we now move this actor along the *x*-coordinate in increments of 0.6, its successive locations will be

12.3, 12.9, 13.5, 14.1, 14.7, 15.3, 15.9, 16.5, 17.1, . . .

and so on. We will see the actor on screen at rounded *x*-coordinates. It will be painted at the following *x*-coordinates

12, 13, 14, 14, 15, 15, 16, 17, 17, . . .

and so on. Altogether, even though it is still rounded to integers for display, the effect is smoother movement than dealing exclusively with `int` fields.

The second bit of functionality that the `SmoothMover` adds is a movement vector. Every object of a subclass of `SmoothMover` holds a vector that indicates a current direction and speed of movement. We can think of a vector as an (invisible) arrow with a given direction and length (Figure 6.4).

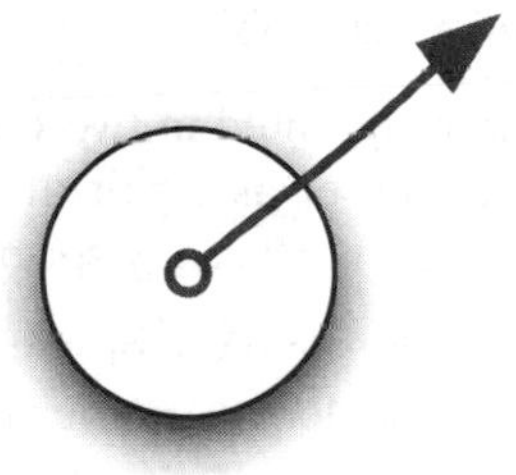

**Figure 6.4**
A `SmoothMover` object with a movement vector

The `SmoothMover` class has methods to change its movement by modifying its movement vector, and a `move` method that moves the actor according to its current vector.

---

**Side note: Abstract classes**

If you right-click the `SmoothMover` class, you will notice that you cannot create objects of this class. No constructor is shown.

When we examine the source code of that class, we can see the keyword **abstract** in the class header. We can declare classes as abstract to prevent creation of instances of these classes. Abstract classes serve only as superclasses for other classes, not for creating objects directly.

---

**Exercise 6.6** Place an object of class **Body** into the world. By examining the object's popup menu, find out what methods this object inherits from class **SmoothMover**. Write them down.

**Exercise 6.7** Which of the method names appears twice? How do the two versions differ?

**Concept:**

**Overloading** is the use of the same method name for two different methods or constructors.

## Terminology: Overloading

It is perfectly legal in Java to have two methods that have the same name, as long as their parameter lists are different. This is called **overloading**. (The name of the method is **overloaded**—it refers to more than one method.)

When we call an overloaded method, the runtime system figures out which of the two methods we mean by examining the parameters we supply.

We also say that the two methods have different *signatures*.

The second helper class, `Vector`, implements the vector itself, and is used by the `SmoothMover` class. Note that `Vector` is not listed in the `Actor` group of classes. It is not an actor—it will never appear in the world on its own. Objects of this class are only ever created and used by other actor objects.

Vectors can be represented in two different ways: either as a pair of distances in their $x$ and $y$ coordinates ($dx$, $dy$) or as a pair of values specifying the direction and its length (direction, length). The direction is usually specified as the angle from the horizontal.

Figure 6.5 shows the same vector with both possible specifications. We see that either the ($dx$, $dy$) pair or the (direction, length) pair can describe the same vector.

**Figure 6.5**

Two possible ways to specify a vector

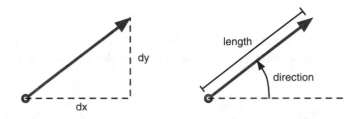

The first representation, using the $x$ and $y$ offsets, is called a *Cartesian* representation. The second, using the direction and length, is a *polar* representation. You will see these two names used in the source code of the `Vector` class.

For our purposes, sometimes the Cartesian representation is easier to use, and sometimes the polar representation is easier. Therefore, our vector class is written in a way that it can deal with both. It will do the necessary conversions internally automatically.

**Exercise 6.8** Familiarize yourself with the methods of the `SmoothMover` and `Vector` classes by opening the editor, and studying their definition in *Documentation* view. (Remember: you can switch to *Documentation* view using the menu in the top right corner of the editor.) You can also read the source code, if you like, but this is not strictly necessary at this stage.

**Exercise 6.9** Place a **Body** object into the world. Which of the methods inherited from `SmoothMover` can you call interactively (through the object's menu)? Which can you not call at this stage?

**6.3** **The existing Body class**

> **Exercise 6.10** Open the source code of the Body class and examine it.

Looking at the source code of the Body class, two aspects are worth discussing a bit further. The first is the fact that the class has two constructors (Code 6.1). This is another example of overloading: It is perfectly legal to have two constructors in a class if they have different parameter lists.

In our case, one constructor has no parameters at all, and the other has four parameters.

**Code 6.1**

Constructors of class Body

```java
public class Body extends SmoothMover
{
    // some code omitted

    private double mass;

    /**
     * Construct a Body with default size, mass, movement and color.
     */
    public Body()
    {
        this (20, 300, new Vector(90, 1.0), defaultColor);
    }

    /**
     * Construct a Body with a specified size, mass, movement and
     * color.
     */
    public Body(int size, double mass, Vector movement, Color color)
    {
        this.mass = mass;
        addForce(movement);
        GreenfootImage image = new GreenfootImage (size, size);
        image.setColor (color);
        image.fillOval (0, 0, size-1, size-1);
        setImage (image);
    }

    // more code omitted
}
```

**Terminology**

A constructor without any parameters is also called a **default constructor**.

The default constructor makes it easy for us to create bodies interactively without having to specify all the details. The second constructor allows creation of a body with custom size, mass, movement, and color. This constructor is used, for example, in the Space class to create the Sun, planet, and Moon.

The second constructor initializes the state of the actor using all its parameter values that have been passed in. The first constructor looks more mysterious. It has only one line of code:

```
this (20, 300, new Vector(90, 1.0), defaultColor);
```

The line looks almost like a method call, except that it uses the keyword this instead of a method name. Using this call, the constructor executes the *other* constructor (the one with the four parameters), and provides default parameters for all the four values. Using the this keyword in this way (like a method name) is only possible within constructors to call another constructor as part of the initialization.

There is a second use of the this keyword:

```
this.mass = mass;
```

Here we have another example of overloading: The same name is used for two variables (a parameter and an instance field). When we assign these values, we need to specify which of these two variables named mass we mean on each side of the assignment.

When we write mass without any qualification, then the closest definition of a variable with that name is used—in this case, the parameter. When we write this.mass, we specify that we mean the mass field of the current object. Thus, this line of code assigns the parameter named mass to the field named mass.

> **Exercise 6.11** Remove the "this." segment before the mass in the line of code shown above, so that it reads
>
> ```
> mass = mass;
> ```
>
> Does this code compile? Does it execute? What do you think this code does? What is its effect? (Create an object and use its Inspect function to examine the mass field. Once finished experimenting, restore the code to how it was before.)

The second aspect that is worth exploring a little further is the two lines near the top of the class, shown in Code 6.2.

**Code 6.2**

Declaration of constants

```
private static final double GRAVITY = 5.8;
private static final Color defaultColor = new Color(255, 216, 0);
```

These two declarations look similar to field declarations, except that they have the two keywords static final inserted after the keyword private.

This is what we call a *constant*. A constant has similarities to a field, in that we can use the name in our code to refer to its value, but the value can never change (it is *constant*). It is the `final` keyword that makes these declaration constants.

The effect of the `static` keyword is that this constant is shared between all actors of this class, and we don't need separate copies of it in every object. We encountered the `static` keyword before (in Chapter 3), in the context of class methods. Just as static methods belong to the class itself (but can be called from objects of that class), static fields belong to the class and can be accessed from its instances.

In this case, the constants declared are a value for gravity[1] (to be used later), and a default color for the bodies. This is an object of type `Color`, which we will discuss in more detail below.

It is good practice to declare fields constant that should not change in a program. Making the field constant will prevent accidental change of the value in the code.

## 6.4   First extension: Creating movement

Okay, enough looking at what's there. It is time to write some code and make something happen.

The first obvious experiment is to make the bodies move. We have mentioned that the `SmoothMover` class provides a `move()` method, and since a `Body` is a `SmoothMover`, it, too, has access to this method.

**Exercise 6.12** Add a call to the `move()` method into the `act` method of `Body`. Test. What is the default direction of movement? What is the default speed?

**Exercise 6.13** Create multiple `Body` objects. How do they behave?

**Exercise 6.14** Call the public `Space` methods (`sunAndPlanet()`, etc.) and run the scenario. How do these objects move? Where are their initial movement direction and speed defined?

**Exercise 6.15** Change the default direction of a body to be toward the left. That is, when a body is created using the default constructor, and its `move()` method is executed, it should move left.

As we see when we perform these experiments, just telling the bodies to move is enough to make them move. They will, however, move in a straight line. This is because movement (speed and direction) is dictated by their movement vector, and currently nothing changes this vector. Thus, movement is constant.

---

[1] Our value of gravity has no direct relationship to any particular unit in nature. It is in an arbitrary unit made up for this scenario. Once we start implementing gravitation for our bodies, you can experiment with different amounts of gravity by changing this value.

## 6.5 Using Java library classes

While reading the code above, in both the `Body` and `Space` classes, we have come across the `Color` class. The second constructor of the `Body` class expects a parameter of type `Color`, and the code in the `Space` class creates `Color` objects with expressions such as

```
new Color(248, 160, 86)
```

The three parameters of the `Color` constructor are the red, green, and blue components of this particular color. Every color on a computer screen can be described as a composite of these three base colors. (We will discuss color a little more in Chapter 8. There, on page 136, you can also find a table of RGB color values. You can use any good graphics program to experiment with these yourself.)

For us, the more pressing question is, where does this class come from? And how can we know what parameters its constructor expects?

A clue to the answer is found near the top of our class, where we can find the line

```
import java.awt.Color;
```

> **Concept:**
>
> The **Java class library** is a large collection of ready-made classes, provided with the Java system. We can use these classes by using an **import** statement.

The class `Color` is one of the many classes from the *Java Standard Class Library*. The Java system comes with a large collection of useful classes which we can just use. Over time, we will get to know many of them.

We can see documentation for all the classes in the class library by selecting *Java Library Documentation* from Greenfoot's *Help* menu. This will open the documentation for the Java libraries in a web browser (Figure 6.6).

The bottom left pane in this window shows a list of all classes in the Java library. (There are many of them!) We can look at the documentation for any particular class by finding it in this list and selecting it. When selected, the main part of the window will display the documentation for this class.

> **Exercise 6.16** Find the class `Color` in the class list. Select it. Look at the documentation of this class. How many constructors does it have?
>
> **Exercise 6.17** Find the description of the constructor we have used (the one with three integers as parameters). What is the legal range for these integer numbers?

You can see that there are literally thousands of classes in the Java library. To get some sort of order into this long list, classes are grouped into *packages*. A package is a group of logically related classes. At the top of the documentation of any class, we can see what package the class is in. The class `Color`, for instance, is in a package called *java.awt*.

When we want to use any of the classes from the Java library in our own scenario, we need to *import* the class, using an import statement as we have seen above. The import statement names the package and the class we want to use, with a dot in between. Thus, to use the `Color` class from the *java.awt* package, we write

```
import java.awt.Color;
```

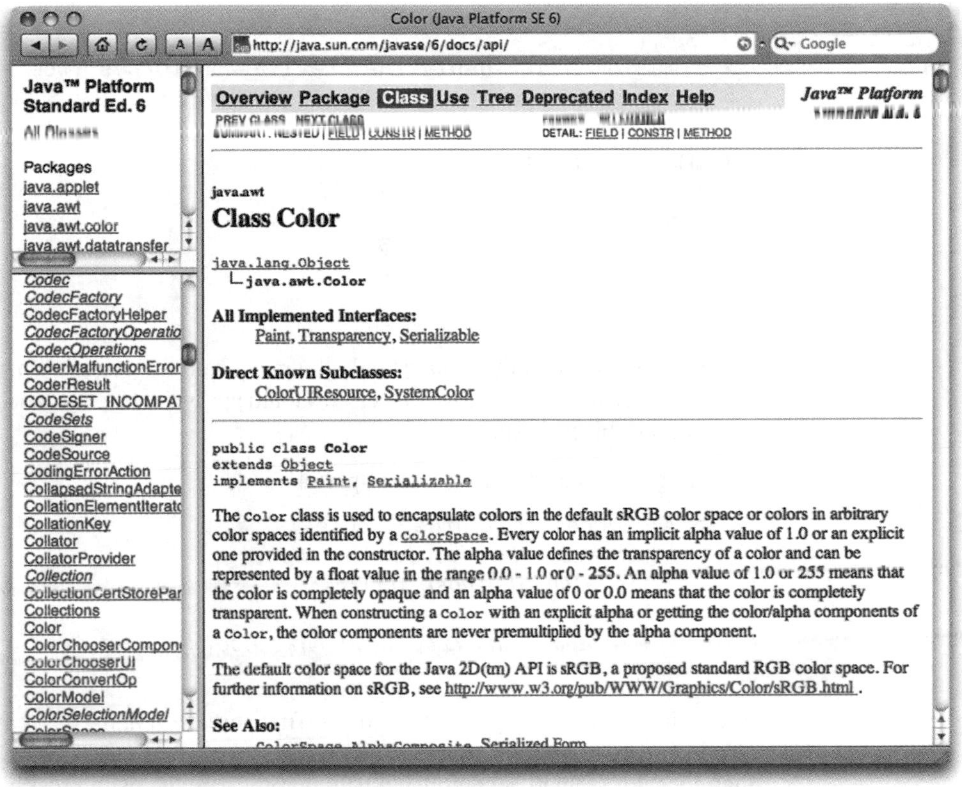

**Figure 6.6**

The *Java Library Documentation*

Importing a class makes it usable within our own scenario, just as if it was one of our own classes. After importing it, we can create objects of this class, call methods, and do anything else we can do with any other class.

The Java library is quite intimidating at first, because it has so many classes. Don't worry—we shall use only a small number of them, and we shall introduce them one by one when we need them.

One of them, however, we need very soon: in the next section.

What we want to do next is to add gravity to this scenario. That is, when we have more than one body in our space, the gravitational pull between these bodies should change each body's movement.

## 6.6 Adding gravitational force

Let us start by looking at the current `act` method in our `Body` class (Code 6.3). (If you have not done Exercise 6.12, then the call to the `move` method will not be there—you can add it now.)

**Code 6.3**

The current `act` method

```java
/**
 * Act. That is: apply the gravitation forces from
 * all other bodies around, and then move.
 */
public void act()
{
    move();
}
```

While the code currently contains only the move call, the comment actually describes correctly what we have to do: Before we move, we should apply the forces caused by the gravitational pull of all other objects in space.

We can give an outline of the task in pseudo-code:

```
apply forces from other bodies:
    get all other bodies in space;
    for each of those bodies:
    {
        apply gravity from that body to our own;
    }
```

Since this is not an easy thing to do, we first start by making a separate method for this task (Code 6.4). Creating a separate (initially empty) method might seem like a trivial task at first that does not seem to accomplish much, but it greatly helps in breaking down our problem into smaller subproblems, and it helps structuring our thoughts.

**Code 6.4**

Preparing to apply forces of gravity

```java
/**
 * Act. For a body, that is: apply all the gravitation forces from
 * all other bodies around, and then move.
 */
public void act()
{
    applyForces();
    move();
}

/**
 * Apply the forces of gravity from all other celestial bodies in
 * this universe.
 */
private void applyForces()
{
    // work to do here
}
```

**Concept:**

**Private methods** are only visible from within the class they are declared in. They are used to improve the structure of the code.

**Note: Private methods**

The method we created in Code 6.4 has the keyword `private` at the beginning of its signature, not `public` as we have previously seen.

Methods can be `public` or `private`. When methods are intended to be called from outside the class (either interactively by a user or from another class), then they must be `public`. When methods are intended to be called only from other methods within the same class (as is the case here), then they should be declared `private`.

`Private` methods are not visible or accessible from outside the class itself. It is good practice to make methods `private` that are only intended for internal use. This helps preventing errors and documents the purpose of the method more clearly.

Next, we have to work out how we get access to all other objects in our world.

The `World` class in Greenfoot has methods that give us access to objects within it.

**Exercise 6.18** Look up Greenfoot's `World` class in the Greenfoot class documentation. Find all methods that give us access to objects within the world. Write them down.

The most interesting of those methods for us is this one:

```
java.util.List getObjects(java.lang.Class cls)
```

This method gives us a list of all objects in the world of a particular class. The parameter to this method is of type `java.lang.Class` (i.e., the class named "Class" from the `java.lang` package[2]). We have seen parameters of this type before, in Chapter 4, when we used the `canSee` and `eat` methods in the `Crab` class to eat the worms. We can use a call to this method to get, for instance, a list of all `Body` objects in our world:

```
getObjects(Body.class)
```

We can also provide `null` as a parameter to receive a list of all objects of any class in the world:

```
getObjects(null)
```

**Concept:**

The keyword **null** stands for "nothing" or "no object".

The keyword `null` is a special expression that means *nothing*, or *no object*. By using it in a parameter list, we pass no object as the parameter. The value `null` could also be assigned to variables.

The `getObjects` method is, however, a method of the `World` class, so it must be called on a `World` object. We will write our code in the `Body` class, so we must first obtain the world object

---

[2] The java.lang package is special: It contains the most commonly used classes, and classes in it are automatically imported. So we do not need to write an import statement for any class in java.lang.

to call this method on. Luckily, there is a method in the `Actor` class that gives us access to the world object. Its signature is

```
World getWorld()
```

Find this method in the Greenfoot class documentation and read its description.

This method will return the world object, and we can then call the `getObjects` method on the resulting object:

```
getWorld().getObjects(Body.class)
```

This code can be used from an actor to get all objects of class `Body`. Let us look more closely at the return type now.

The return type of the `getObjects` method is specified as `java.util.List`. This indicates that there is a type called `List` in the `java.util` package in the standard class library, and that we will get an object of this type as a result of this method.

The `List` type is worth a closer look.

## 6.7 The List type

**Concept:**

A **collection** is a kind of object that can hold many other objects.

**Concept:**

A **List** is an example of a collection. Some methods from the Greenfoot API return List objects.

Dealing with collections of objects is important both in Greenfoot programming and in programming in general. Several of the Greenfoot methods return collections of objects as their result, usually in the form of a list. The type of the returned object then is the `List` type from the `java.util` package.

> **Side Note: Interfaces**
>
> The `List` type is a little different from other object types we have seen: It is not a class, but an *interface*. Interfaces are a Java construct that provides an abstraction over different possible implementing classes. The details are not important to us right now—it is sufficient to know that we can deal with the `List` type in similar ways as with other types: We can look it up in the Java Library Documentation, and we can call the existing methods on the object. We cannot, however, create objects directly of type `List`. We will come back to this issue later.

> **Exercise 6.19** Look up `java.util.List` in the Java Library Documentation. What are the names of the methods used to add an object to the list, remove an object from the list, and to find out how many objects are currently in the list?

> **Exercise 6.20** What is the proper name of this type, as given at the top of the documentation?

When we looked at the `getObjects` method in the previous section, we noticed that it returns an object of type `java.util.List`. Thus, in order to store this object, we need to declare a variable of this type. We will do this in our `applyForces` method.

The List type, however, is different from other types we have seen before. The documentation shows at the top

```
Interface List<E>
```

Apart from the word *interface* in place of *class*, we notice another new notation: the <E> after the type name.

Formally, this is called a *generic type*. This means that the type List needs an additional type specified as a parameter. This second type specifies the type of the elements held within the list.

For example, if we are dealing with a list of strings, we would specify the type as

```
List<String>
```

If instead we are dealing with a list of actors, we can write

```
List<Actor>
```

In each case, the type within the angle brackets (<>) is the type of some other known kind of object. In our case, we expect a list of bodies, so our variable declaration will read:

```
List<Body> bodies
```

Now we can assign the list which we retrieve from the getObjects method to this variable:

```
List<Body> bodies = getWorld().getObjects(Body.class);
```

After executing this line, our variable bodies holds a list of all bodies that currently exist in the world (see also Code 6.5). (Remember that you must also add an import statement for java.util.List at the top of your class.)

**Code 6.5**

Getting a list of all bodies in space

```
private void applyForces()
{
    List<Body> bodies = getWorld().getObjects(Body.class);
    ...
}
```

## 6.8 The for-each loop

The next step we have to achieve, now that we have a list of all bodies, is to apply the gravitational force from each body to our movement.

We will do this by going through our list of bodies one by one, and applying the force from each body in turn.

Java has a specialized loop for stepping through every element of a collection, and we can use this loop here. It is called a *for-each* loop, and it is written using the following pattern:

```
for (ElementType variable : collection)
{
    statements;
}
```

In this pattern, *ElementType* stands for the type of each element in the collection, *variable* is a variable that is being declared here, so we can give it any name we like, *collection* is the name of the collection we wish to process, and *statements* is a sequence of statements we wish to carry out. This will become clearer with an example.

Using our list named `bodies`, we can write

```
for (Body body : bodies)
{
    body.move();
}
```

(Remember that Java is case sensitive: `Body` with an uppercase "B" is different from `body` with a lowercase "b". The uppercase name refers to the class, the lowercase name refers to a variable holding an object. The plural version—`bodies`—is another variable that holds the whole list.)

We can read the *for-each* loop a little more easily if we read the keyword `for` as "for each", the colon as "in", and the opening curly bracket as "do". This then becomes

```
for each body in bodies do:...
```

This reading also gives us a hint as to what this loop does: It will execute the statements in the curly brackets once for each element in the list `bodies`. If, for example, there are three elements in that list, the statements will be executed three times. Every time, before the statements are executed, the variable `body` (declared in the loop header) will be assigned one of the list elements. Thus, the sequence of action will be

```
body = first element from 'bodies';
execute loop statements;
body = second element from 'bodies';
execute loop statements;
body = third element from 'bodies';
execute loop statements;
...
```

The variable `body` is available to be used in the loop statements to access the current element from the list. We could then, for example, call a method on that object, as in the example shown above, or pass the object on to another method for further processing.

We can now use this loop to apply gravity from all other bodies to this one:

```
for (Body body : bodies)
{
    applyGravity(body);
}
```

In this code, we just take each element (stored in the variable `body`) and pass it to another method named `applyGravity`, which we will have to write in a moment.

We should add one more thing: Since `bodies` is a list of all bodies in space, it includes the current object (the one we want to apply gravity to) as well. We do not need to apply gravity of an object to itself, so we can add an `if` statement that calls `applyGravity` only if the element from the list is not the current object itself.

The result is shown in Code 6.6. Note how the keyword `this` is used here to refer to the current object.

**Code 6.6**

Applying gravity from all other bodies in space

```java
private void applyForces()
{
    List<Body> bodies = getWorld().getObjects(Body.class);

    for (Body body : bodies)
    {
        if (body != this)
        {
            applyGravity (body);
        }
    }
}

/**
 * Apply the gravity force of a given body to this one.
 */
private void applyGravity(Body other)
{
    // work to do here
}
```

## 6.9 Applying gravity

In Code 6.6, we have solved the task of accessing each object in space, but we have deferred the task of actually applying the gravitational force. The method `applyGravity` (another example of a private method) still needs to be written.

This is now a little easier than before, though, since this method now only needs to deal with two objects at a time: the current object, and one other object specified in its parameter. We now want to apply the gravitational force from the other object to this one. This is where Newton's Law comes into play.

Newton's formula for gravitation looks like this:

$$\text{force} = \frac{\text{mass1} \times \text{mass2}}{\text{distance}^2} \, G$$

In other words, to calculate the force we need to apply to the current object, we need to multiply the mass of this object with the mass of the other object, and then divide by the square of the distance between the two objects. Finally, the value gets multiplied by the constant G—the *Gravitational Constant*. (You may remember that we have already defined a constant for this value in our class, named *GRAVITY*.)

If you are very confident or adventurous, you may like to try to implement the `applyGravity` method yourself. You need to create a vector in the direction from the current body to the other body, with a length specified by this formula. For the rest of us, we now look at the finished implementation of that method (Code 6.7).

**Code 6.7**

Calculating and applying gravity from another body

```java
/**
 * Apply the gravity force of a given body to this one.
 */
private void applyGravity(Body other)
{
    double dx = other.getExactX() - this.getExactX();
    double dy = other.getExactY() - this.getExactY();
    Vector force = new Vector (dx, dy);
    double distance = Math.sqrt (dx * dx + dy * dy);
    double strength = GRAVITY * this.mass * other.mass /
                        (distance * distance);
    double acceleration = strength / this.mass;
    force.setLength (acceleration);
    addForce (force);
}
```

This method is not quite as complicated as it looks. First, we calculate the distances between our object and the other object in the $x$ and $y$ coordinates ($dx$ and $dy$). Then we create a new vector using these values. This vector now has the right direction, but not the correct length.

Next, we calculate the distance between the two objects using the *Pythagoras theorem* ($a^2 + b^2 = c^2$ in right-angled triangles, see Figure 6.7).

**Figure 6.7**

The distance in relation to *dx* and *dy*

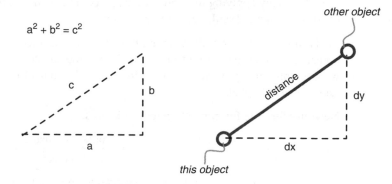

$$a^2 + b^2 = c^2$$

This tells us that the distance is the square root of $dx$ squared plus $dy$ squared. In our code (Code 6.7), we use a method called `sqrt` from the `Math` class to calculate the square root. (`Math` is a class in java.lang, and thus automatically imported.)

**Exercise 6.21** Look up the class `Math` in the Java documentation. How many parameters does the `sqrt` method have? What types are they? What type does this method return?

**Exercise 6.22** In the Math class, find the method that can be used to find the maximum of two integers. What is it called?

The next line in our code calculates the strength of the force by using Newton's formula of gravitation given above.

The final thing to do is to calculate the acceleration, since the actual movement change to our object is not only determined by the force of gravity, but also the mass of our object: The heavier the object, the slower it will accelerate. Acceleration is computed using the following formula:

$$\text{acceleration} = \frac{\text{force}}{\text{mass}}$$

Once we have calculated the acceleration, we can set our force vector to the correct length and add this vector to the movement of our body. Doing this is easy, using the `addForce` method that is provided by the `SmoothMover` class.

**Exercise 6.23** Map the variables in Code 6.7 to Newton's formula, the Pythagoras theorem, and the acceleration formula given above. Which variable corresponds to which part of which formula?

With this, our task is completed. (An implementation of the code described so far is also available in the book scenarios as *Newtons-Lab-2*.)

This task clearly involved more background knowledge in math and physics than the others we have seen. If this is not your favorite area, don't worry, we shall return to less mathematical projects shortly. Remember: programming can do anything you like. You can make it very mathematical, but you can also make it very creative and artistic.

## 6.10 Trying it out

Now that we have completed our implementation of gravitational forces, it is time to try it out. We can start by using the three ready-made scenarios defined in the `Space` class.

**Exercise 6.24** With your completed gravity code, try out the three initialization methods from the `Space` object again (`sunAndPlanet()`, `sunAndTwoPlanets()`, and `sunPlanetMoon()`). What do you observe?

**Exercise 6.25** Experiment with changes in gravity (the `GRAVITY` constant at the top of the `Body` class).

**Exercise 6.26** Experiment with changes to the mass and/or initial movement of the bodies (defined in the `Space` class).

**Exercise 6.27** Create some new set-ups of stars and planets and see how they interact. Can you come up with a system that is stable?

**Pitfall**

Be careful when using the constructor of class `Vector`. The constructor is overloaded: one version expects an `int` and a `double` as parameters, the other expects two `doubles`. Thus

```
new Vector(32, 12.0)
```

will call one constructor, while

```
new Vector(32.0, 12.0)
```

will call the other constructor, resulting in an entirely different vector.

You will quickly see that it is very hard to configure the parameters so that the system remains stable for a long time. The combination of mass and gravity will often result in objects crashing into each other, or escaping from orbit. (Since we have not implemented a "crashing into each other", our objects can essentially fly through each other. However, when they get very close, their force becomes very large and they often catapult each other onto strange trajectories.)

Some of these effects are similar to nature, although our simulation is a little inaccurate due to some simplifications we have made. The fact, for example, that all objects act in sequence, rather than simultaneously, will have an effect on the behavior and is not a realistic representation. To make the simulation more accurate, we would have to calculate all forces first (without moving) and then execute all moves according to the previous calculations. Also, our simulation does not model the forces accurately when two bodies get very close to each other, adding more unrealistic effects.

We can also ask the stability question about our own solar system. While the orbits of the planets in our solar system are quite stable, precise details about their movement are hard to predict accurately for a long time into the future. We are quite certain that none of the planets will crash into the Sun in the next few billion years, but small variations in orbit may happen. Simulations such as ours (just much more accurate and detailed, but similar in principle) have been used to try to predict the future orbits. We have seen, however, that this is very hard to simulate accurately. Simulations can show that minute differences in the initial conditions can make huge differences after a few billion years[3].

---

[3] If you are interested to read more, Wikipedia is a good starting point: http://en.wikipedia.org/wiki/Stability_of_the_solar_system

Seeing how difficult it is to come up with parameters that create a system that is stable even for a limited time, we might be surprised that our solar system is as stable as it is. But there is an explanation: When the solar system formed, material from a gas cloud surrounding the Sun formed into lumps that slowly grew by colliding with other lumps of matter and combining to form ever-growing objects. Initially, there were countless of the lumps in orbit. Over time, some fell into the Sun, some escaped into deep space. This process ends when the only chunks left are well separated from one another and on generally stable orbits.

It would be possible to create a simulation that models this effect. If we correctly model the growth of planets out of billions of small, random lumps of matter, we would observe the same effect: Some large planets form that are left in fairly stable orbits. For this, however, we would need a much more detailed and complicated simulation and a lot of time: Simulating this effect would take a very, very long time, even on very fast computers.

## 6.11 Gravity and music

Before we leave our *Newton's Lab* scenario behind, we have one more thing to play with: adding music. Well, noise, in any case.[4]

The idea is as follows: We add a number of *Obstacles* into our world. When obstacles are touched by our planets, they make a sound. Then we create a few planets or stars, let them fly around, and see what happens.

We will not discuss this implementation in detail. Instead, we leave you to study it yourself, and just point out some of the more interesting features. You can find an implementation of this idea in the book scenarios as *Newtons-Lab-3*.

> **Exercise 6.28** Open the scenario named *Newtons-Lab-3* and run it. Have a look at the source code. Try to understand how it works.

Here is a summary of the most interesting changes we have made from the previous version to create this:

- We have added a new class `Obstacle`. You can easily see objects of this class on screen. Obstacles have two images: the orange rectangle you see most of the time, and a lighter version of the rectangle to show when they are touched. This is used to create the "lighting up" effect. Obstacles are also associated with a sound file, just as the piano keys were in our piano scenario. In fact, we are reusing the sound files from the piano scenario here, so they do sound the same.

- We have modified the Body class so that bodies bounce off the edges off the screen. This gives a better effect for this kind of scenario. We have also increased gravity a bit to get faster

---

[4] The idea to add sound to a gravity project was inspired by *Kepler's Orrery* (see https://keplers-orrery. dev.java.net/ or search for "Kepler's Orrery" on YouTube).

movement and modified the code so that bodies automatically slow down once they get too fast. Otherwise they might speed each other up more and more indefinitely.

■ Finally, we have added code in the `Space` class to create a fixed row of obstacles, and to create five random planets (random size, mass, and color).

The implementation of these three changes includes a few interesting snippets of code that are worth pointing out.

■ In the `Obstacle` class, we use a method named `getOneIntersectingObject` to check whether the obstacle is being hit by a planet. The code pattern is the following:

```
Object body = getOneIntersectingObject(Body.class);
if (body != null)
{
    ...
}
```

The `getOneIntersectingObject` method is defined in class `Actor`, and is available to all actors. It will return an actor that this one intersects with if there is such an actor, or `null` if no other actor intersects with this one. The following `if` statement that checks whether `body` is null is therefore a check whether any other object intersected this one.

This is an example of *collision detection*, and we will discuss more of it in the next chapter.

■ In the `Space` class, we have added two methods, `createObstacles` and `randomBodies`. The first creates the obstacles with their associated sound file names, quite similar to the initialization code in the piano example. The second uses a `while` loop to create a number of `Body` objects. The bodies are initialized with random values. The `while` loop counts down from a given number to 0, to create the right number of objects. It is worth studying as another example of a loop.

---

**Exercise 6.29** Change the number of bodies that are created by default in this scenario.

**Exercise 6.30** Play with the movement parameters to see whether you can create nicer movement for the planets. The parameters are: the value for **GRAVITY**; the acceleration value used when bouncing off an edge (currently 0.9); the speed threshold (currently 7) and acceleration (0.9) used in the **applyForces** method to slow down fast objects; and the initial mass used for the planets (in the **Space** class).

**Exercise 6.31** Create a different arrangement of obstacles in your scenario.

**Exercise 6.32** Use different sounds (different sound files) for your obstacles.

**Exercise 6.33** Use different images for your obstacles.

**Exercise 6.34** Make planets change color every time they bounce off the edge of the universe.

**Exercise 6.35** Make planets change color every time they hit an obstacle.

**Exercise 6.36** Make a different kind of obstacle that gets switched on and off by being hit. When on, it continuously blinks and produces a sound at fixed intervals.

**Exercise 6.37** Add some keyboard control. For example, pressing the right arrow key could add a small force to the right to all **Body** objects.

**Exercise 6.38** Allow adding more planets. A mouse click into the universe while it is running should create a new planet at that location.

There are countless other possible ways to make this scenario more interesting and nicer to look at. Invent some of your own and implement them!

## 6.12 Summary of programming techniques

In this chapter, we have touched on a number of new concepts. We have seen a new scenario— Newton's Lab—that simulates stars and planets in space. Simulations in general are a very interesting topic, and we will come back to them in Chapter 9.

We have seen two useful helper classes, `SmoothMover` and `Vector`, both of which help us to create more sophisticated movement.

One of the most important new topics in this chapter was the use of additional classes from the standard Java class library. We have used `Color`, `Math`, and `List` from the library. We will come back to this with the use of more classes in the remaining chapters.

Another new addition to our tool set was the use of a new loop: the *for-each* loop. This loop is used to do something to every element of a Java collection, such as a list. This is another bit of code that we will need to use again later.

*For-each* loops are especially useful when processing objects from a collection. However, they cannot be used without a collection, and they do not provide an index while processing the elements. If we need an index, or a loop independent of a collection, then we must use a `for` loop or a `while` loop instead.

And finally, we have seen some more useful methods from the Greenfoot API, such as the `getObjects` method from the `World` class and the `getOneIntersectingObject` method from the `Actor` class. The last one leads us into the more general area of collision detection, which we shall discuss in more detail in the next chapter, where we pick up the *Asteroids* game again.

## Concept summary

■ **Overloading** is the use of the same method name for two different methods or constructors.

■ The keyword **this** is used to call one constructor from another, or to refer to the current object.

■ A **constant** is a named value that can be used in similar ways as a variable, but can never change.

■ The **Java class library** is a large collection of ready-made classes, provided with the Java system. We can use these classes by using an **import** statement.

■ **Private methods** are only visible from within the class they are declared in. They are used to improve the structure of the code.

■ The keyword **null** stands for "nothing" or "no object".

■ A **collection** is a kind of object that can hold many other objects.

■ A **List** is an example of a collection. Some methods from the Greenfoot API return List objects to us.

■ A **generic type** is a type that receives a second type name as a parameter.

■ The **for-each loop** is another kind of loop. It is well suited to process all elements of a collection.

■ The Greenfoot API contains methods for **collision detection**. These make it possible to detect when one actor touches another. (More about this in the next chapter.)

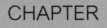
# Collision detection: Asteroids

| topics: | more about movement, keyboard control and collision detection |
|---|---|
| concepts: | collections (again), for loop, for-each loop (again), casting |

In this chapter, we shall not introduce many new concepts, but instead revisit and deepen our understanding of some topics we have touched on in the last couple of chapters. We shall revisit a scenario that we have encountered before, very early in this book: Asteroids (Figure 7.1).

The version of Asteroids that we use here is slightly different than the one we looked at earlier. It has some added features (such as a proton wave and a score counter), but it is not fully implemented.

**Figure 7.1**
The new Asteroids scenario (with proton wave)

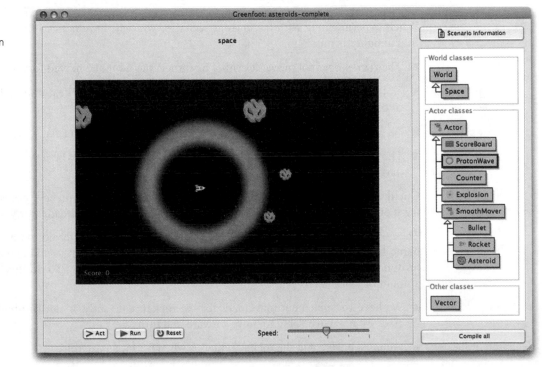

Important parts of the functionality are still missing, and it will be our job in this chapter to implement them.

We shall use this example to revisit movement and collision detection. In terms of Java programming concepts, we will use this to gain more practice with loops and collections.

## 7.1 Investigation: What is there?

We should start this project by examining the existing code base. We have a partially implemented solution, named *asteroids-1*, in the *chapter07* folder of the book scenarios. (Make sure to use the *chapter07* version, not the copy from *chapter01*.)

**Exercise 7.1** Open the *asteroids-1* scenario from the *chapter07* folder of the book projects. Experiment with it to find out what it does, and what it does not do.

**Exercise 7.2** Write down a list of things that should be added to this project.

**Exercise 7.3** Which keyboard key is used to fire a bullet?

**Exercise 7.4** Place an explosion into a running scenario (by interactively creating an object of class `Explosion`). Does it work? What does it do?

**Exercise 7.5** Place a proton wave into a scenario. Does this work? What does it do?

When experimenting with the current scenario, you will have noticed that some fundamental functionality is missing:

- The rocket does not move. It cannot be turned, nor can it be moved forward.

- Nothing happens when an asteroid collides with the rocket. It flies straight through it, instead of damaging the rocket.

- As a result of this, you cannot lose. The game never ends, and a final score is never displayed.

- The `ScoreBoard`, `Explosion`, and `ProtonWave` classes, which we can see in the class diagram, do not seem to feature in the scenario.

One thing that we can do, however, is fire bullets at asteroids. (If you have not yet found out how, try it out.) Asteroids break up when hit by a bullet or, if they are already fairly small, disappear.

The goal of this game would obviously be to clear the screen of asteroids without our rocket ship being hit itself. To make it a little more interesting, we also want to add another weapon—the proton wave. And we want to keep a score while we're playing. To do this, we have a good amount of work to do.

- We have to implement movement for the rocket. Currently, it can fire bullets, but nothing else. We need to be able to move forward and turn.

- We must ensure that the rocket explodes when we hit an asteroid.

- When the rocket explodes, we want to put up a scoreboard that displays our final score.

- We want to be able to release a proton wave. The proton wave should start small around the rocket ship and then gradually spread out, destroying asteroids when it hits them.

But before we get into these functions, we start with one more minor cosmetic thing: Painting stars into our universe.

## 7.2 Painting stars

In all our previous scenarios, we used a fixed image as the background for the world. The image was stored in an image file in our file system.

In this scenario, we'd like to introduce a different technique to make background images: painting them on the fly.

The Asteroid scenario does not use an image file for the background. A world that does not have a background image assigned will, by default, get an automatically created background image that is filled with plain white.

> **Exercise 7.6** Investigate the constructor of the **Space** class in your scenario. Find the lines of code that create the black background.

Looking at the *asteroids-1* scenario, we can see that the background is plain black. When we investigate the constructor of the **Space** class, we can find these three lines of code:

```
GreenfootImage background = getBackground();
background.setColor(Color.BLACK);
background.fill();
```

> **Exercise 7.7** Remove these three lines from your class. You can do this by just commenting them out. What do you observe? (Once done, put them back in.)

**Tip:**
If you want to remove some code temporarily, it is easier to "comment it out", rather than deleting it. The Greenfoot editor has a function to do this. Just select the lines in question, and invoke 'Comment' (F8) or 'Uncomment' (F7) from the *Edit menu*.

The first line retrieves the current background image from the world. This is the automatically generated (white) image. We then have a reference to the world background stored in the background variable.

The background object that we have stored here is of class GreenfootImage—we have seen this class before.

> **Exercise 7.8** Look up the documentation for the class GreenfootImage. What is the name of the method used to draw a rectangle? What is the difference between drawOval and fillOval?

The second line in the code fragment above sets the paint color to black. Doing this has no immediate effect (it does not change the color of the image). Instead, it determines the color that is used by all following drawing operations. The parameter is a constant from the Color class, which we encountered in the previous chapter.

> **Exercise 7.9** Look up the documentation of class Color again. (Do you remember which package it is in?) For how many colors does this class define constant fields?

The third line of the code fragment now fills our image with the chosen color. Note that we do not need to set this image again as the background of the world. When we got the image (using getBackground()), we got a reference to the background image, and the same image still remains the world background. It is not removed from the world just because we now have a reference to it.

When we paint onto this image, we are painting directly onto the background of the world.

Our task now is to draw some stars onto the background image.

> **Exercise 7.10** In class Space, create a new method named **createStars**. This method should have one parameter of type **int**, named **number**, to specify the number of stars it should create. It has no return value. The method body should—for now—be empty.
>
> **Exercise 7.11** Write a comment for the new method. (The comment should describe what the method does, and explain what the parameter is used for.)
>
> **Exercise 7.12** Insert a call to this new method into your **Space** constructor. 300 stars may be a good amount to start with (although you can later experiment with different numbers and choose something that you think looks good).
>
> **Exercise 7.13** Compile the class Space. At this stage, you should not see any effect (since our new method is empty), but the class should compile without problems.

**Concept:**

The **for loop** is one of Java's loop constructs. It is especially good for iterating a fixed number of times.

In the createStars method, we will now write code to paint some stars onto the background image. The exact amount of stars is specified in the method's parameter.

We will use yet another loop to achieve this: the *for* loop.

Previously, we have seen the *while loop* and the *for-each loop*. The *for loop* uses the same keyword as the *for-each loop* (for), but has a different structure. It is

```
for (initialization; loop-condition; increment)
{
    loop-body;
}
```

An example of this loop can be seen in the addAsteroids method in the Space class.

> **Exercise 7.14** Examine the `addAsteroids` method in class **Space**. What does it do?
>
> **Exercise 7.15** Look at the `for` loop in that method. From the loop header, write down the *initialization* part, the *loop-condition*, and the *increment*. (See the definition of the `for` loop above.)

The initialization part of a `for` loop is executed exactly once before the loop starts. Then the loop condition is checked: If it is true, the loop body is executed. Finally, after the loop body has been completely executed, the increment section from the loop header is executed. After this, the loop starts over: The condition is evaluated again and, if true, the loop runs again. This continues until the loop conditions returns false. The initialization is never executed again.

A `for` loop could quite easily be replaced by a `while` loop. A `while` loop equivalent of the `for` loop structure shown above is this:

```
initialization;
while (loop-condition)
{
    loop-body;
    increment;
}
```

The `while` loop structure shown here and the `for` loop structure shown above do exactly the same thing. The main difference is that, in the `for` loop, the initialization and the increment have been moved into the loop header. This places all elements that define the loop behavior in one place, and can make loops easier to read.

The `for` loop is especially practical if we know at the beginning of the loop already how often we want to execute the loop.

The `for` loop example found in the `addAsteroids` method reads

```
for (int i = 0; i < count; i++)
{
    int x = Greenfoot.getRandomNumber(getWidth()/2);
    int y = Greenfoot.getRandomNumber(getHeight()/2);
    addObject(new Asteroid(), x, y);
}
```

This shows a typical example of a `for` loop:

- The initialization part declares and initializes a loop variable. This variable is often called `i`, and often initialized to 0.

- The loop condition checks whether our loop variable is still less than a given limit (here: `count`). If it is, the loop will continue.

- The increment section simply increments the loop variable.

Different variations of the `for` loop are possible, but this example shows a very typical format.

**Exercise 7.16** In your `Space` class, rewrite the `for` loop in `addAsteroids` as a `while` loop. Make sure that it does the same as before.

**Exercise 7.17** Rewrite this method again with a `for` loop, as it was before.

**Exercise 7.18** Implement the body of the `createStars` method that you created earlier. This method should include the following:

- Retrieve the world's background image.
- Use a `for` loop similar to the one in `addAsteroids`. The limit for the loop is given in the method parameter.
- In the body of the loop, generate random **x** and **y** coordinates. Set the color to white and then paint a filled oval with a width and height of two pixels.

Test! Do you see stars in your world? If all went well, you should.

**Exercise 7.19** Create stars of random brightness. You can do this by creating a random number between 0 and 255 (the legal range for RGB values for colors) and creating a new `Color` object using the same random value for all three color components (red, green, and blue). Using the same value for all color components ensures that the resulting color is a shade of neutral gray. Use this new random color for painting the stars. Make sure to generate a new color for every new star.

These exercises are quite challenging. If you have trouble, you can look into the solution. An implementation of this is provided in the *asteroids-2* version of this scenario. Alternatively, you can ignore this section for now, continue with the following tasks first, and come back to this later.

## 7.3 Turning

In the previous section, we spent a lot of effort just on looks. We used a `for` loop to create the stars in the background. That was hard work for little effect. However, knowing the `for` loop will come in very handy later.

Now, we want to achieve some real functionality: We want to make the rocket move. The first step to this is to make it turn when the right or left arrow key is pressed on the keyboard.

**Exercise 7.20** Examine the `Rocket` class. Find the code that handles keyboard input. What is the name of the method that holds this code?

**Exercise 7.21** Add a statement that makes the rocket rotate left while the "left" key is pressed. In every act cycle, the rocket should rotate 5 degrees. You can use the `getRotation` and `setRotation` methods from the `Actor` class to achieve this.

> **Exercise 7.22** Add a statement that makes the rocket rotate right while the "right" key is pressed. Test!

If you managed to successfully complete the exercises, your rocket should be able to turn now when you press the arrow keys. Since it fires in the direction it is facing, it can also fire in all directions.

The next challenge is to make it move forward.

## 7.4 Flying forward

Our Rocket class is a subclass of the SmoothMover class, which we have already seen in the previous chapter. This means that it holds a movement vector that determines its movement, and that it has a move() method that makes it move according to this vector.

Our first step is to make use of this move() method.

> **Exercise 7.23** In the Rocket's act method, add a call to the move() method (inherited from SmoothMover). Test. What do you observe?

Adding the call to move() to our act method is an important first step, but does not achieve much by itself. It causes the rocket to move according to its movement vector, but since we have not initiated any movement, this vector currently has length 0, so no movement takes place.

To change this, let us first introduce a small amount of automatic drift, so that the rocket starts off with some initial movement. This makes it more interesting to play, because it stops players from being able to just remain stationary for a long time.

> **Exercise 7.24** Add a small amount of initial movement to the rocket in its constructor. To do this, create a new vector with some arbitrary direction and a small length (I used 0.3 for my own version) and then use the **SmoothMover**'s addForce method with this vector as a parameter to add this force to the rocket. (Make sure to use an **int** as your first parameter in the Vector's constructor, in order to use the correct constructor.)
>
> Test. If all went well, the rocket should drift all by itself when the scenario starts. Don't make this initial drift too fast. Experiment until you have a nice, slow initial movement.

Next, we want to add movement controls for the player. The plan is that pressing the "up" arrow key ignites the rocket's booster and moves us forward.

For the other keyboard input, we have used code of the following pattern:

```
if (Greenfoot.isKeyDown("left"))
{
    setRotation(getRotation() - 5);
}
```

For the movement forward, we need a slightly different pattern. The reason is that, for the rotation shown here, we need to act only if the key is being pressed.

The movement forward is different: When we press the "up" key to move, we want to change the rocket's image to show the rocket engine firing. When we release the key, the image should return to the normal image. Thus, we need a code pattern along these lines:

```
when "up" key is pressed:
    change image to show engine fire;
    add movement;

when up key is released:
    change back to normal image;
```

Showing the images is quite easy. The scenario already contains two different rocket images for this: *rocket.png* and *rocketWithThrust.png*. Both images are loaded into fields toward the top of the Rocket class.

Since we need to react in both cases, when the "up" key is pressed and when it is not pressed, we will define and call a separate method to handle this functionality.

In checkKeys, we can insert the following method call:

```
ignite(Greenfoot.isKeyDown("up"));
```

We can then write a method called ignite that does the following:

■ It receives a boolean parameter (say, boosterOn) that indicates whether the booster should be on or off.

■ If the booster is on, it sets the image to *rocketWithThrust.png* and uses addForce to add a new vector. This vector should get its direction from the current rotation of the rocket (getRotation()) and have a small, constant length (say, 0.3).

■ If the booster is not on, set the image to *rocket.png*.

**Exercise 7.25** Add the call to the ignite method to your checkKeys method, exactly as shown above.

**Exercise 7.26** Define a method stub (a method with an empty body) for the ignite method. This method should have one boolean parameter, and a void return type. Make sure to write a comment. Test! The code should compile (but not do anything yet).

**Exercise 7.27** Implement the body of the ignite method, as outlined in the bullet points above.

For the implementation of our ignite method, it is okay if the image gets set every time the method is called, even when it is not necessary (e.g., if the booster is off, and it was also off last time, we would not need to set the image again since it has not changed). Setting the image even when it is not strictly necessary has very little overhead and so avoiding it is not crucial.

Once you have completed these exercises, you have reached a stage where you can fly your rocket around and fire at asteroids.

A version of the project that implements the exercises presented so far in this chapter is provided as *asteroids-2* in the book scenarios.

## 7.5 **Colliding with asteroids**

The most obvious fault with our asteroids game at this stage is that we can fly right through the asteroids. That leaves not much of a challenge to play this game, since we cannot lose. We shall fix that now.

The idea is that our rocket ship should explode when we crash into an asteroid. If you did the exercises earlier in this chapter, then you have already seen that we have a fully functional Explosion class available in our project. Simply placing an explosion into the world will show an adequate explosion effect.

Thus, a rough description of the task to solve is this:

```
if (we have collided with an asteroid) {
    remove the rocket from the world;
    place an explosion into the world;
    show final score (game over);
}
```

Before we look into solving these subtasks, we prepare our source code to implement this task, as we did before with other functionality. We follow the same strategy as before: Since this is a separate subtask, we shall put it into a separate method, in order to keep our code well structured and easily readable. You should usually start the implementation of new functionality like this. The next exercise achieves this.

**Exercise 7.28** Create a new method stub (a method with an empty body) in class Rocket for checking for collisions with asteroids. Call it checkCollision. This method can be private and needs no return value and no parameters.

**Exercise 7.29** In the Rocket's act method, add a call to the checkCollision method. Ensure that your class compiles and runs again.

**Concept:**

Greenfoot provides several methods for **collision detection**. They are in the Actor class.

The first subtask is to check whether we have collided with an asteroid. Greenfoot's Actor class contains a number of different methods to check for collisions with different functionality.

Appendix C presents a summary of the different collision detection methods and their functionality. This might be a good time to have a quick look through it. At some stage, you should become familiar with all the collision detection methods.

For our purpose `getIntersectingObjects` seems like a good fit. Two objects intersect if any of the pixels in their images intersect. This is pretty much what we need.

There is one small problem: transparent pixels in the actor images.

Images in Greenfoot are always rectangles. When we see non-rectangular images, such as the rocket, this is because some pixels in the image are *transparent* (invisible; they contain no color). For the purpose of our program, however, they are still part of the image.

> **Concept:**
>
> The **bounding box** of an image is the enclosing rectangle of that image.

Figure 7.2 shows the rocket and asteroid images with their *bounding boxes*. The bounding box is the edge of the actual image. (The image of the rocket is a little bigger than what seems necessary to make it the same size as the second rocket image, *rocketWithThrust*, which shows the flame in the currently empty area.)

In Figure 7.2, the images intersect, even though their visible parts do not touch. The collision detection methods will report this as an intersection. They work with the bounding boxes, and pay no attention to the non-transparent parts of the image.

As a result, our rocket will make "contact" with an asteroid even though, on screen, there seems to be still a little distance between them.

For our asteroids game, we choose to ignore this. Firstly, the distance is small, so often players will not notice. Secondly, it is easy enough to come up with a story line to explain this effect ("flying too close to an asteroid destroys your ship because of the gravitational pull").

Sometimes it would be nice to check whether the actual visible (non-transparent) parts of an image intersect. This is possible, but much more difficult. We will not discuss this here.

Now that we have decided to go with intersection, we can look at the `Actor` methods again. There are two methods for checking object intersection. Their signatures are

```
List getIntersectingObjects(Class cls)
Actor getOneIntersectingObject(Class cls)
```

Both methods accept a parameter of type `Class` (which means that we can check for intersections with a specific class of object if we want to). The difference is that one method will return a list of all objects that we currently intersect with, while the other returns only a single object. In case we intersect more than one other object, the second method randomly chooses one of them and returns it.

**Figure 7.2**
Two actor images and their bounding boxes

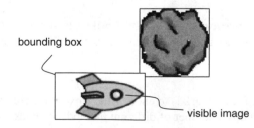

bounding box

visible image

For our purpose, the second method is good enough. It actually makes no difference to the game whether we crash into one asteroid, or into two of them simultaneously. The rocket will explode just the same. The only question for us is, did we intersect with any asteroid at all?

Thus, we shall use the second method. Since it returns an `Actor`, rather than a `List`, it is slightly simpler to work with. It will return an actor if we do have an intersection, or `null` if we currently do not intersect with any asteroid. We can check for a `null` return value to see whether we crashed into anything:

```
Actor a = getOneIntersectingObject(Asteroid.class);
if (a != null)
{
    ...
}
```

**Exercise 7.30** Add a check for intersecting with an asteroid, similar to the one shown here, to your own `checkCollision` method.

**Exercise 7.31** Add code to the body of the `if` statement that adds an explosion to the world at the current position of the rocket, and removes the rocket from the world. (To do this, you need to use the `getWorld()` method to access its methods for adding and removing objects from the world.)

For the last exercise above, we can use our own `getX()` and `getY()` methods to retrieve our current position. We can use this as the coordinates for placing the explosion.

An attempt at solving this might look like this:

```
World world = getWorld();
world.removeObject(this); // remove rocket from world
world.addObject(new Explosion(), getX(), getY());
```

This code looks reasonable at first glance, but will not work.

**Exercise 7.32** Try out the code as shown above. Does it compile? Does it run? At what point does something go wrong, and what is the error message?

The reason this does not work is that we are calling the `getX()` and `getY()` methods after removing the rocket from the world. When an actor is removed from the world, it does not have any coordinates anymore—it has coordinates only while being in the world. Thus, the `getX()` and `getY()` method calls fail in this example.

This can easily be fixed by switching the last two lines of code: Insert the explosion first, and then remove the rocket from the world.

**Exercise 7.33** This is a very advanced exercise, and you may want to skip it initially, and come back to it later.

The explosion used here is a fairly simple looking explosion. It is good enough for the moment, but if you want to create really good looking games, it can be improved. A more sophisticated way to show explosions is introduced in a Greenfoot tutorial video, available on the Greenfoot web site:

```
http://www.greenfoot.org/doc/videos.html
```

Create a similar explosion for your rocket.

## 7.6 Casting

Our game is now fairly playable. You may have noticed that the score counting does not work (we will look into that later), and that nothing happens when you lose. Next, we shall add a big "Game Over" sign at the end, when the rocket crashes.

This is almost easy to do: There is already a `ScoreBoard` class in the project that we can use.

**Exercise 7.34** Create an object of class `ScoreBoard` and place it into the world.

**Exercise 7.35** Examine the source code of the `ScoreBoard` class. How many constructors does it have? What is the difference between them?

**Exercise 7.36** Modify the `ScoreBoard` class: Change the text shown on it; change the color of the text; change the background and frame colors; change the font size so that your new text fits well; change the width of the scoreboard to suit your text.

As you have seen, the scoreboard includes a "Game over" text and the final score (although the score is currently not correctly counted, but we shall worry about that later).

The `Space` class already has a method, named `gameOver`, that is intended to create and show a scoreboard.

**Exercise 7.37** Find and examine the `gameOver` method in the `Space` class. What does its current implementation do?

**Exercise 7.38** Implement the `gameOver` method. It should create a new `ScoreBoard` object, using the constructor that expects an `int` parameter for the score. For now, use 999 as the score—we will fix this later. Place the scoreboard into the world, exactly centered in the middle.

So, it seems most of the work has been well prepared for us. We now only need to call the gameOver method when we want the game to finish.

The place in our code where we want the game to be over is in our rocket's `checkCollision` method: If we detect a collision, the rocket should explode (we have done that) and the game is over.

Simply adding the gameOver call creates a problem. This is quite a fundamental problem, and we need to examine it in more detail. Let us look at the code so far, assuming we just add a call to the gameOver method to our checkCollision (Code 7.1). This code will not compile.

**Code 7.1**
A first attempt at calling the gameOver method

```
private void checkCollision()
{
    Actor a = getOneIntersectingObject(Asteroid.class);
    if (a != null)
    {
        World world = getWorld();
        world.addObject(new Explosion(), getX(), getY());
        world.removeObject(this); // remove rocket from world
        world.gameOver(); // error: this will not work
    }
}
```

When trying to compile this code, we get an error message that reads

*cannot find symbol—method gameOver()*

This message is trying to tell us that the compiler cannot find a method with this name. We know, however, that such a method exists in our Space class. We also know that the getWorld() call used here gives us a reference to our Space object. So what is the problem?

The problem lies in the fact that the compiler is not quite as smart as we would like. The getWorld() method is defined in class Actor, and its signature is this:

```
World getWorld()
```

We can see that it states that it will return an object of type World. The actual world that it returns in our case is of type Space.

**Concept:**

Objects can be of **more than one type**: the type of their own class, and the type of the class's superclass.

This is not a contradiction: Our world object can be of type World and of type Space at the same time, because Space is a subclass of World (Space *is a* World; we also say that the type Space is a *subtype* of type World).

The error comes from the difference between the two: gameOver is defined in class Space, while getWorld gives us a result of type World. The compiler looks only at the return type of the method we are calling (getWorld). Because of this, the compiler searches for the gameOver method only there and it does not find it. That's why we get the error message.

To solve this problem, we need to tell the compiler explicitly that this world we're getting is actually of type Space. We can do this by using a *cast*.

```
Space space = (Space) getWorld();
```

**Concept:**

**Casting** is the technique of specifying a more precise type for our object than the one the compiler knows about.

*Casting* is the technique of telling the compiler a more precise type for our object than it can work out for itself. In our case, the compiler can work out that the object returned from getWorld is of type World, and we are now telling it that it is actually of class Space. We do this by writing the class name (Space) in parentheses before the method call. Once we have done this, we can call methods defined in Space:

```
space.gameOver();
```

It is worth noting that casting does not change the type of the object. Our world actually is of type Space all along. The problem is just that the compiler does not know this. With the cast, we are just giving additional information to the compiler.

Back to our checkCollision method. Once we have cast our world to Space and stored it in a variable of type Space, we can call all methods on it: those defined in Space and those defined in World. Thus, our existing calls to addObject and removeObject should still work, and the gameOver call should work as well.

**Exercise 7.42** Implement the call to the gameOver method, using the cast of the World object to Space, as discussed here. Test. This should now work, and the scoreboard should come up when the rocket explodes.

**Exercise 7.43** What happens when you use a cast incorrectly? Try casting the world object to, say, Asteroid instead of Space. Does this work? What do you observe?

This work so far has achieved the display of our "Game Over" sign (still with an incorrect score). We shall leave the scoring as an exercise at the end of this chapter. If you really want to fix this now, you may like to jump ahead to the end-of-chapter exercises and look into this first. Here, we will look at proton waves next.

## 7.7 Adding fire power: The proton wave

Our game is getting pretty good. The final thing we shall discuss in detail in this chapter is the addition of a second weapon: the proton wave. This should give the game a little more variety. The idea is this: Our proton wave, once released, radiates outward from our rocket ship, damaging or destroying every asteroid in its path. Since it works in all directions simultaneously, it is a much more powerful weapon than our bullets. For the game, we should probably restrict how often or how frequently you can use it, so that the game does not become too easy to play.

> **Exercise 7.44** Run your scenario. Place a proton wave into the scenario—what do you observe?

The exercise shows us that we have a proton wave actor, which shows the wave at full size. However, this wave does not move, does not disappear, and does not cause any damage to asteroids.

Our first task will be to make the wave grow. We will start it very small, and then grow it until it reaches the full size that we have just seen.

> **Exercise 7.45** Examine the source code of class `ProtonWave`. What are the methods that already exist?
>
> **Exercise 7.46** What is the purpose of each method? Review the comments of each method and expand them to add a more detailed explanation.
>
> **Exercise 7.47** Try to explain what the `initializeImages` method does and how it works. Explain in writing, using diagrams if you like.

## 7.8 Growing the wave

We have seen that the `ProtonWave` class has a method—`initializeImages`—that creates 30 images of different sizes and stores them in an array (Code 7.2). This array, named `images`, holds the smallest image at index 0, and the largest one at index 29 (see Figure 7.3). The images are created by loading a base image (*wave.png*) and then, in a loop, creating copies of this image and scaling them to different sizes.

**Code 7.2**

Initializing the images for the proton wave

```
/**
 * Create the images for expanding the wave.
 */
public static void initializeImages()
{
    if(images == null)
    {
        GreenfootImage baseImage = new GreenfootImage("wave.png");
        images = new GreenfootImage[NUMBER_IMAGES];
```

**Code 7.2 continued**

Initializing the images for the proton wave

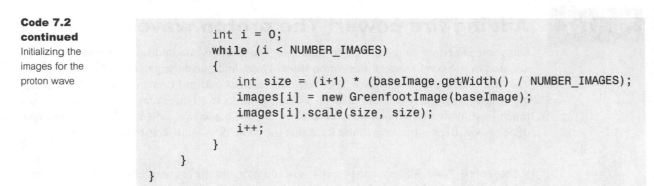

```
int i = 0;
while (i < NUMBER_IMAGES)
{
    int size = (i+1) * (baseImage.getWidth() / NUMBER_IMAGES);
    images[i] = new GreenfootImage(baseImage);
    images[i].scale(size, size);
    i++;
}
}
}
```

**Figure 7.3**

An array of images (some left out for space reasons)

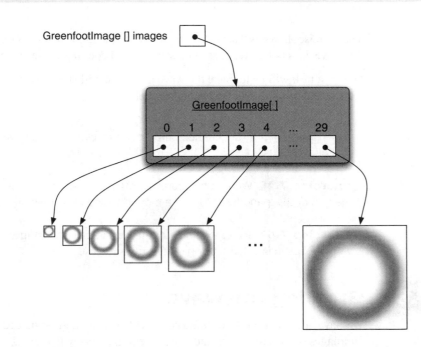

This method uses the `scale` method from the `GreenfootImage` class to do the scaling. It also uses a `while` loop for the iteration. However, this is an example where a `for` loop, which we encountered at the beginning of this chapter, might be appropriate.

**Exercise 7.48** Rewrite the `initializeImages` method to use a `for` loop instead of a `while` loop.

In practice, it is not very important which loop to use in this case. (We changed it here mainly to gain additional practice in writing `for` loops.) This is, however, a case where a `for` loop is a good choice, because we have a known number of iterations (the number of images) and we can make good use of the loop counter in calculating the image sizes. The advantage over the `while` loop is that the `for` loop brings all elements of the loop (initialization, condition, and increment) together in the header, so that we run less danger of forgetting one of its parts.

The images field and the initializeImages method are static (they use the static keyword in their definition). As we have briefly mentioned in Chapter 7, this means that the images field is stored in the ProtonWave *class*, not in the individual instances. As a result, all objects that we shall create of this class can share this set of images, and we do not need to create a separate set of images for each object. This is much more efficient than using a separate image set each time.

Copying and scaling these images takes a fairly long time (between a tenth of a second and half a second on a current average computer). This does not may seem very much, but it is long enough to introduce a visible, annoying delay when we do it in the middle of playing a game. To solve this, the code of this method is enclosed in an if statement:

```
if (images == null)
{
    ...
}
```

This if statement ensures that the main part of this method (the body of the if statement) is executed only once. The first time, images will be null, and the method executes fully. This will initialize the images field to something other than null. From then on, the test of the if statement is all that will be executed, and the body will be skipped. The initializeImages method is actually called every time a proton wave is created (from the constructor), but only the very first time it is called, substantial work will be done.[1]

Now that we have a fair idea of the code and the fields that already exist, we can finally get to work and make something happen.

What we want to do is the following:

- We want to start the wave off with the smallest image.
- At every act step, we want to grow the wave (show the next larger image).
- After we have shown the largest image, the wave should disappear (be removed from the world).

The following exercises will achieve this.

**Exercise 7.49** In the constructor of class ProtonWave, set the image to the smallest image. (You can use images[0] as the parameter to the setImage method.)

**Exercise 7.50** Create an instance field named imageCount of type int, and initialize it to 0. We will use this field to count through the images. The current value is the index of the currently displayed image.

---

[1] The method is actually called for the first time from the Space constructor, so it executes even before the first proton wave is created. This avoids a delay for the first proton wave as well. The call is included in the proton wave constructor only as a safety feature: If this class is ever used in another project, and this method is not called in advance, all will still work.

**Exercise 7.51** Create a method stub for a new private method called `grow`. This method has no parameter and does not return a value.

**Exercise 7.52** Call the `grow` method from your `act` method. (Even though it does not do anything at this stage.)

We're almost there. The only thing left is to implement the `grow` method. The idea, roughly, is this:

```
show the image at index imageCount;
increment imageCount;
```

We will also have to add an `if` statement that first checks whether `imageCount` has exceeded the number of images. In that case, we can remove the proton wave from the world and we're done.

**Exercise 7.53** Implement the `grow` method along the lines discussed above.

**Exercise 7.54** Test your proton wave. If you interactively create a proton wave and place it into the world while the scenario is running, you should see the wave expansion effect.

**Exercise 7.55** Add some sound. A sound file named *proton.wav* is included with the scenario—you can just play it. You can place the statement to play the sound into the constructor of the proton wave.

Now that we have a functioning proton wave, we should equip our rocket to release it.

**Exercise 7.56** In class `Rocket`, create a method stub named `startProtonWave` without parameters. Does it need to return anything?

**Exercise 7.57** Implement this method: It should place a new proton wave object into the world, at the current coordinates of the rocket.

**Exercise 7.58** Call this new method from the `checkKeys` method when the "z" key is pressed. Test.

**Exercise 7.59** You will quickly notice that the proton wave can be released much too often now. For firing the bullets, a delay has been built into the `Rocket` class (using the `gunReloadTime` constant and the `reloadDelayCount` field). Study this code and implement something similar for the proton wave. Try out different delay values until you find one that seems sensible.

## 7.9 Interacting with objects in range

We now have a proton wave that we can release at a press of a button. The remaining problem is: This proton wave does not actually do anything to the asteroids.

We now wish to add code that causes damage to the asteroids when they get hit by the proton wave.

> **Exercise 7.60** Prepare for this new functionality: In class **ProtonWave**, add a method stub for a method called **checkCollision**. The method has no parameters and does not return a value. Call this method from your **act** method.
>
> **Exercise 7.61** The purpose of this new method is to check whether the wave touches an asteroid, and cause damage to it if it does. Write the method comment.

This time we do not want to use the `getIntersectingObjects` method, since the invisible image areas at the corners of the proton wave image (included in the bounding box, but not part of the blue-ish circle) are fairly large, and asteroids would be destroyed long before the wave seems to reach them.

Instead, we will use another collision detection method, called `getObjectsInRange`.

The `getObjectsInRange` method returns a list of all objects within a given radius of the calling object (see Figure 7.4). Its signature is

```
List getObjectsInRange(int radius, Class cls)
```

When called, we can specify the class of objects we are interested in (as before), and we also specify a radius (in cells). The method will then return a list of all objects of the requested class that are found within this radius around the calling object.

To determine which objects are within the range, the center points of objects are used. For example, an asteroid would be within range 20 of a rocket if the distance of its center point to

**Figure 7.4**

The range around an actor with a given radius

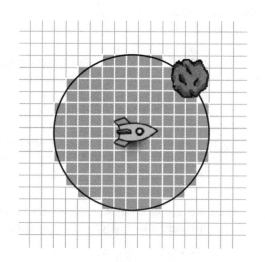

the center point of the rocket is less than 20 cell widths. The size of the image is not relevant for this method.

Using this method, we can implement our `checkCollision` method.

Our proton wave will have images of increasing size. At each act cycle, we can use the size of the current image to determine the range of our collision check. We can find out our current image size using the following method calls:

```
getImage().getWidth()
```

We can then use half of this size as our range (since the range is specified as a radius, not a diameter).

> **Exercise 7.62** In `checkCollision`, declare a local variable named *range* and assign half the current image width to it.
>
> **Exercise 7.63** Add a call to `getObjectsInRange` that returns all asteroids within the calculated range. Assign the result to a variable of type `List<Asteroid>`. Remember that you also have to add an import statement for the `List` type.

These exercises give us a list of all asteroids in the range of the proton wave. We now want to do some damage to each asteroid in range.

The `Asteroid` class has a method called `hit` that we can use to do this. This method is already being used to do damage to the asteroid when it is hit by a bullet, and we can use it again here.

We can use a for-each loop to iterate through all asteroids in the list we received from the `getObjectsInRange` call. (If you are unsure about writing for-each loops, look back to Section 6.8.)

> **Exercise 7.64** Find the `hit` method in the `Asteroid` class. What are its parameters? What does it return?
>
> **Exercise 7.65** The `ProtonWave` class has a constant defined toward the top, called DAMAGE, that specifies how much damage it should cause. Find the declaration of this constant. What is its value?
>
> **Exercise 7.66** In method `checkCollision`, write a for-each loop that iterates over the asteroid list retrieved from the `getObjectsInRange` call. In the loop body, call `hit` on each asteroid using the DAMAGE constant for the amount of damage caused.

Once you have completed these exercise, test. If all went well, you should now have a playable version of this game that lets you shoot at asteroids and also release proton waves to destroy many asteroids in one go. You will notice that you should make the reload time for the proton wave quite long, since the game gets too easy if you can use the wave too often.

This version of the game, including all the changes made in the last few sections, is available in the book projects as *asteroids-3*. You can use this version to compare it to your own scenario, or to look up solutions if you get stuck in one of the exercises.

## 7.10 Further development

We are at the end of the detailed discussion of development of this scenario in this chapter. There are, however, a large number of further improvements possible to this game. Some are quite obvious, others you may like to invent yourself.

Following are some suggestions for further work, in the form of exercises. Many of them are independent of each other—they do not need to be done in this particular order. Pick those first that interest you most, and come up with some extensions of your own.

**Exercise 7.67** Fix the score counting. You have seen that there already is a score counter, but it is not being used yet. The counter is defined in class `Counter`, and a counter object is being created in the `Space` class. You will have to do roughly the following: Add a method to the `Space` class named something like `countScore`—this should add a score to the score counter; and call this new method from the `Asteroid` class whenever an asteroid gets hit (you may want to have different scores for splitting the asteroid and removing the last little piece).

**Exercise 7.68** Add new asteroids when all have been cleared. Maybe the game should start with just two asteroids, and every time they are cleared away, new ones appear, one more every time. So in the second round, there are three asteroids, in the third round four, etc.

**Exercise 7.69** Add a level counter. Every time the asteroids are cleared, you go up a level. Maybe you get higher scores in later levels.

**Exercise 7.70** Add an end-of-level sound. This should be played every time a level is completed.

**Exercise 7.71** Add an indicator showing the load state for the proton wave, so that the player can see when it is ready to be used again. This could be a counter, or some sort of graphical representation.

**Exercise 7.72** Add a shield. When the shield is deployed, it stays there for a short fixed time. While the shield is up, it can be seen on screen, and colliding asteroids do no damage.

There are, of course, countless more possible extensions. Invent some of your own, implement them, and submit your results to the Greenfoot Gallery.

## 7.11 Summary of programming techniques

In this chapter, we have worked on completing an asteroids game that was initially half-written. In doing this, we have encountered several important constructs again that we had seen before, including loops, lists, and collision detection.

We have seen one new style of loop—the `for` loop—and we have used it to paint the stars, and to generate the proton wave images. We have also revisited the for-each loop when we implemented the proton wave functionality.

Two different collision detection methods were used: `getOneIntersectingObject` and `getObjectsInRange`. Both have their advantages in certain situations. The second one of those returned a list of actors to us, so we had to deal with lists again.

Understanding lists and loops is initially quite difficult, but very important in programming, so you should carefully review these aspects of your code if you are not yet comfortable in using them. The more practice you get, the easier it becomes. After using them for a while, you will be surprised that you found them so difficult at first.

### Concept summary

- The **for loop** is one of Java's loop constructs. It is especially good for iterating a fixed number of times.

- Greenfoot provides several methods for **collision detection**. They are in the Actor class.

- The **bounding box** of an image is the enclosing rectangle of that image.

- Objects can be of **more than one type**: the type of their own class, and the type of the class's superclass.

- **Casting** is the technique of specifying a more precise type for our object than the one the compiler knows about.

# The Greeps competition

We will take a little time out to go on a second interlude—a break in the chapter sequence to do something a little different. This time, we will look at "Greeps"—a programming competition.

The Greeps are alien creatures. And they've come to Earth! One of the important things to know about Greeps is that they like tomatoes. They have landed with their spaceship and are swarming out to find and collect tomatoes (Figure I2.1).

**Figure I2.1**

Two Greeps hunting for tomatoes

The challenge in this programming competition will be to program your Greeps so that they find and collect tomatoes as quickly as possible. You will have limited time, and every tomato you manage to bring back to the spaceship scores a point.

You can do this project as a competition against a friend who programs their own Greeps, or you can do it as a contest for a whole group of programmers, such a school class. If you're on your own, you could post your entry to the Greenfoot Gallery and see how you compare to other people there.[1] Or you could do it on your own just for the fun of it—either way, it should be an interesting challenge.

---

[1] If you submit the Greeps scenario to the Greenfoot Gallery, please do not include source code. We want to keep this project as a challenge to future programmers and don't want to make it too easy to find solutions of others.

## I2.1  How to get started

To start, open the *greeps* scenario from the *book-scenarios* folder. Run this scenario.

You will see that a spaceship lands in an area with sand and water. The Greeps will leave the spaceship and start searching for tomato piles (which happen to be found in various places in this area). Greeps are land animals—they cannot and will not walk into the water. (In fact, they are so sensitive to water that they dissolve very quickly in it, so don't try.)

When you try out the scenario, you will quickly see that the Greeps do not behave very intelligently. They head out in a random direction from the ship, but when they reach the edge of the water, they will just stay there, because they cannot go forward.

Your task will be to program the Greeps to use some more intelligent strategy, so that they find the tomatoes and bring them back to the ship.

There are some facts about the Greeps that will be good to know:

■ There are 20 Greeps in the spaceship. They will come out after landing to start their work. You cannot get any more of them.

■ Greeps can carry a tomato on their back, but they cannot load tomatoes onto their own back. They can only load a tomato *onto another Greep's* back! This means, that two of them have to be at the tomato pile at the same time to pick up a tomato.

**Figure I2.2**

A tribe of Greeps using paint drops

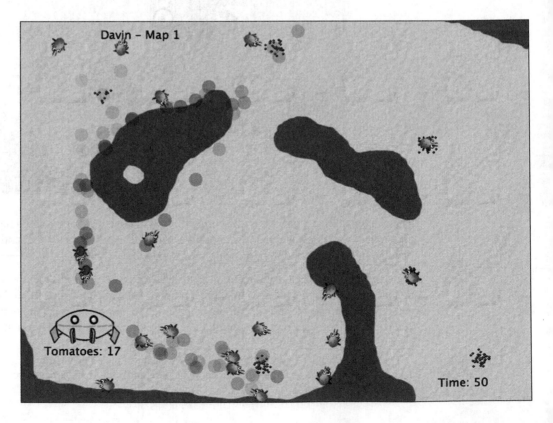

- Greeps cannot talk, or communicate verbally in any way. They can, however, spit paint onto the ground. And they can spit in three different colors! There are rumors that there once was a tribe of Greeps who used this to convey information to each other.

- Greeps are very short sighted. They can only see the ground at their immediate location, and cannot look any further.

- Greeps have a good memory—they never forget what they know. However—unfortunately— their memory is very limited. They can only remember a few things at a time.

Armed with this extensive background knowledge, we can now get ready to program our Greeps.

## 12.2 Programming your Greeps

To program your Greeps to collect as many tomatoes as possible, you should improve their behavior. The Greep class, which is included in the scenario, already includes some behavior (albeit not very clever) that you can look at to get started.

We can see that Greep is a subclass of Creature. Class Creature provides a number of very useful methods that we can use.

There are, however, a number of rules that you must follow:

**Rule 1:** *Only change the class "Greep". No other classes may be modified or created.*

**Rule 2:** *You cannot extend the Greeps' memory. That is, you are not allowed to add fields (other than final fields) to the class. Some general purpose memory (one int and two booleans) is provided.*

**Rule 3:** *You cannot move more than once per "act" round.*

**Rule 4:** *Greeps do not communicate directly. They do not call each other's methods or access each other's fields.*

**Rule 5:** *No long vision. You are allowed to look at the world only at the immediate location of the Greep. Greeps are almost blind, and cannot look any further.*

**Rule 6:** *No creation of objects. You are not allowed to create any scenario objects (instances of user-defined classes, such as Greep or Paint). Greeps have no magic powers—they cannot create things out of nothing.*

**Rule 7:** *No teleporting. Methods from Actor that cheat normal movement (such as setLocation) may not be used.*

It is important to follow these rules. It is technically easy to break them, but that is considered cheating.

To program your Greeps, you work mainly in the Greeps' act method (and any other private methods you choose to create).

Some tips to get started:

- Read the documentation of class Creature. (The best way to do this is to open the class in the editor and switch to Documentation view.) These are some of the most useful methods for your work. Know what is there.

- Work in small steps. Start making small improvements and see how it goes.

- Some first improvements could be as follows: turn around when you are at water; wait if you find a tomato pile (and try to load tomatoes); turn if you are at the edge of the world; . . .

You will soon figure out many more improvements you can do. It gets especially interesting once you start using the paint drops on the ground to make marks for other Greeps to find.

## 12.3 Running the competition

It helps to have a judge who runs the competition. In a school, this might be your teacher. If you run this with friends, it could be a selected person (who then cannot take part as a normal contestant in the competition himself).

To make the competition interesting, there should be two versions of the Greeps scenario. One gets handed out to all contestants. (This is the one included in the book scenarios.) This scenario includes three different maps. The Greeps land and forage on each of the three maps in turn. (So the challenge for contestants is to develop movement algorithms that are flexible enough to work on different maps, not just a known one.)

The judge should have a different scenario that includes more maps. We recommend running the competition with 10 different maps. Contestants do not get access to the last seven maps—they can only test on the first three. Then they hand in their Greeps for scoring, and the judge then runs the contestants' Greeps on all 10 maps (maybe on a large display screen) to reach the official score.

The competition is best run over several days (or maybe a week or two), with repeated chances for contestants to submit their work for scoring, so that they can slowly improve.

## 12.4 Technicalities

For submission of an entry to the judge, the easiest mechanism is that contestants submit only the *Greeps.java* file. The judge then copies that file into his full (10-map) scenario, recompiles, and runs it. This ensures that no other classes are modified in the process.

Some artwork (to make flyers or posters for the competition) is available at

    http://www.greenfoot.org/competition/greeps/

Instructors can also find instructions there for obtaining a version of the Greeps scenario with 10 maps. Alternatively, instructors can make more maps themselves fairly easily. An image of an empty map is provided in the *images* folder of the Greeps scenario. Water can just be painted onto the map, and map data (location of tomato piles, etc.) can be specified in the Earth class.

CHAPTER

# 8

# Creating images and sound

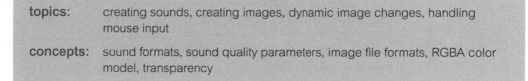

| | |
|---|---|
| **topics:** | creating sounds, creating images, dynamic image changes, handling mouse input |
| **concepts:** | sound formats, sound quality parameters, image file formats, RGBA color model, transparency |

Many of the scenarios we have encountered previously were interesting not only because of the program code that defined their behavior, but also because they made effective use of sound and images. So far, we have not discussed the production of these media files much, and have mostly relied on existing pictures and sounds.

In this chapter, we shall discuss some aspects of creating and managing these media files. We first discuss some background about sound in computer programs, followed by various techniques to create and handle images.

As a side effect, we shall also encounter dealing with mouse input.

## 8.1 Preparation

In contrast to previous chapters, we will not build a complete scenario in this chapter but work through various smaller exercises that illustrate separate techniques that can then be incorporated into a wide variety of different scenarios. The first sequence of exercises guides us through creating a scenario which plays a sound—which we create ourselves—when the user clicks on an actor.

For these exercises, we shall not use a prepared, partly implemented starting scenario this time but create a new one from scratch.

---

**Exercise 8.1** As a preparation for the exercises in this chapter, create a new scenario. You can call it anything you like.

You will see that the new scenario automatically includes the `World` and `Actor` superclasses, but no other classes.

**Exercise 8.2** Create a subclass of `World`. Call it `MyWorld`. You can give it any background image you like. Compile.

**Exercise 8.3** Change the size and resolution of the world so that it has a cell size of one pixel, and a size of 400 cells width and 300 cells height.

**Exercise 8.4** Create an actor subclass in your scenario. At this stage, it does not matter much what it is. You may like to look through the available library images shown in the *New class* dialog, and choose one that looks interesting. Name your class appropriately. (Remember: class names should start with a capital letter.)

**Exercise 8.5** Add code to your `MyWorld` class that automatically places an instance of your actor into the world.

**Exercise 8.6** Write code into your actor's **act** method that moves the actor 10 pixels to the right every time it acts.

You should now have a scenario with an actor that moves to the right when you run it. Movement, however, is not our main goal here. We added movement only to have an initial visual effect to experiment with.

The next step in our preparation will be to make the actor react to mouse clicks.

**Exercise 8.7** In class `Greenfoot`, there are several methods that can handle mouse input. What are they? Look them up in the Greenfoot Class Documentation and write them down.

**Exercise 8.8** What is the difference between `mouseClicked` and `mousePressed`?

When we want to react to mouse clicks, we can use the `mouseClicked` method from the `Greenfoot` class. This method returns a boolean and can be used as a condition in an `if` statement.

The parameter to the `mouseClicked` method can specify an object that the mouse was clicked on. We can pass `null` as the parameter if we do not care where the mouse was when it was clicked—the method will then return true if the mouse was clicked anywhere.

**Exercise 8.9** Modify the code in your actor class so that it only moves to the right in reaction to a mouse click. The mouse click can be anywhere in the world.

**Exercise 8.10** Now modify your code so that the actor only moves when the user clicks on the actor. To do this, you have to pass the actor itself (instead of `null`) as a parameter to the `mouseClicked` method. Remember, you can use the keyword `this` to refer to the current object.

**Exercise 8.11** Test your code: Place multiple instances of your actor into the world and make sure that only the one you click on moves.

You should now have a scenario with an actor that can react to mouse clicks. This is a good starting point for our following experiments with sound and images. (If you had trouble creating this, there is a scenario called *soundtest* in the book scenarios for this chapter that implements this starting point.)

## 8.2 Working with sound

As we have already seen earlier, the `Greenfoot` class has a `playSound` method that we can use to play a sound file. To be playable, the sound file must be located in the *sounds* folder inside the scenario folder.

As a start, let us play an existing sound file.

**Exercise 8.12** Select a sound file from one of your other Greenfoot scenarios and copy it into the *sounds* folder of your current scenario. Then modify your actor so that it plays the sound (instead of moving) when you click on it.

### Pitfall

Some operating systems are configured so that file name suffixes (extensions) are not displayed. A file that is fully named *mysound.wav* would then be displayed only as *mysound*. This is a problem, because we need to use the full name, including the suffix, from our Java code. Writing

```
Greenfoot.playSound("mysound");
```

would fail, because the file would not be found. However, without seeing the suffix, we have no idea what it is.

The solution is to change the operating system's settings so that suffixes are always displayed. Windows, for example, has a checkbox titled *Hide extensions for known file types*, and you should make sure that this is not checked. In Windows Vista, you can find this checkbox by looking at your folder's contents and going through the menus *Organize/Folder and Search Options/View*. In other Windows systems, the menu names may vary, but the checkbox will be there as well.

We can easily play an existing sound file. The more interesting task now is to make sound file ourselves.

## 8.3 Sound recording and editing

There are various different options for obtaining sound files. We can copy sounds from other Greenfoot projects, or download them from various free sound libraries on the Internet. If you copy sounds form the Internet, pay attention to copyright notices: Not everything that is on the Internet is free—respect other people's copyright! The easiest option to obtain sound files is to record them ourselves.

To do this, we need a microphone (many laptops have microphones built in, and often computer headsets have microphones attached) and sound recording software. If you do not have a microphone available right now, you may want to skip this section.

Many sound recording programs are available, several of them are free. We will use *Audacity*[1] here for the sample screenshots. Audacity is a good choice because it is powerful, runs on different operating systems, and is free and fairly easy to use. There are many other sound recording programs, however, so feel free to use one of your own choice.

Figure 8.1 shows a typical interface of a sound recording program. You typically have controls for recording, playback, etc., and a wave form display of the recorded sound (the blue graph).

**Figure 8.1**
A sound recording and editing program (Audacity)

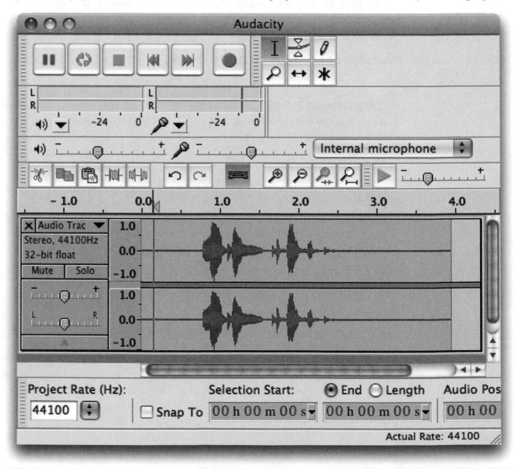

---

[1] Audacity is available from http://audacity.sourceforge.net

Recording the sound is pretty straight forward—you can usually figure this out by playing with the program for a little while.

**Exercise 8.13** Open a sound recording program and record a sound. Play it back. Does it come out as you expected? If not, delete it and try again.

When we record sounds, we often have a few seconds at the beginning and the end of our recording that we do not want. Most sound recording programs allow us to edit the sound before saving, so we can cut off the bits that we don't need.

In Figure 8.1, for example, we can see a fairly long time of silence at the beginning and the end of the sound file (the straight horizontal lines on the left and right end of the graph). If we save the sound file as it is, the effect would be that the sound seems delayed when we play it (since the first part of the sound that gets played is a second of silence).

We can edit the sound by selecting parts of it and using cut, copy, and paste to remove or copy selected parts.

**Exercise 8.14** Edit your sound file so that it includes only the exact sound you want. Remove any noise or silence at the beginning or end, or any parts in the middle that are not needed.

Many sound editing programs also offer filters to modify the sound or to generate entirely new sound elements. Using filters, many different sound effects can be generated. By applying effects, such as amplification, echoes, reverting, speed changes, and others, to simple sounds (such as clapping, whistling, shouting, etc.), we can create a wide variety of effects.

**Exercise 8.15** If your sound program supports filters, apply some filters to your recorded sound. Select three of your favorite filters and describe, in writing, what they do. Describe an example where you might use this effect.

**Exercise 8.16** Produce the following sounds: a rabbit chewing a carrot; an explosion; a sound of two hard objects colliding; a "game over" sound where the player has lost the game; an "end of game" sound used when the player has won; a robot voice; and a "jumping" sound (used when a game character jumps).

When the editing of the sound is complete, we are ready to save it to a file.

## 8.4 Sound file formats and file sizes

Sound files can be saved in many different formats and in different encodings, and this can get quite confusing very quickly.

Greenfoot can play sounds saved in WAV, AIFF, and AU formats. (No MP3 files, I'm afraid.) These formats, however, are what is known as "envelope formats"—they can contain different encodings,

**Concept:**

Sounds can be saved in a variety of different **formats** and **encodings**. Not all programs can play all sound formats. For Greenfoot, we usually use **WAV** format.

and Greenfoot can read only some of them. As a result, Greenfoot cannot, for example, play all WAV files.

When you save your own recorded sounds, you should save them as a "signed 16 bit PCM WAV" file. This is the safest format to ensure playback. In many sound recording programs, this is achieved by using an "Export" function, rather than the standard "Save" function. Make sure to save in this format.

When you come across sound files that Greenfoot cannot play (maybe downloaded from the Internet), you can usually open them in your sound editing program and convert them to this format.

**Exercise 8.17** Save your recorded sound in an appropriate format for Greenfoot. Move the sound file into the *sounds* folder of your scenario. Modify the code of your actor class so that it plays your sound when it is clicked.

**Exercise 8.18** Modify your code so that it plays one sound effect when clicked with the left mouse button, and another sound effect when clicked with the right mouse button. To do this, you need to get information about the mouse click that tells you which button was pressed. Greenfoot has methods to achieve this—study the Greenfoot class documentation to find out how this can be done.

**Exercise 8.19** Modify your code so that the actor, when it is clicked, plays a sound effect and moves to a new random location.

**Concept:**

The **sample format**, **sample rate,** and **stereo/mono** setting of a sound recording determine file size and sound quality.

Sound files can quickly become very large. This is not a major problem as long as the scenario is only used locally, but if the scenario is exported, for instance to the Greenfoot Gallery, then the size can make a big difference. Sound and image files are often the largest parts of a Greenfoot scenario, and the sound file sizes can make all the difference between a scenario loading quickly and users having to wait for minutes for a scenario to download.

To avoid overly large sound files, we should pay attention to encoding details. When we record and save sounds, we can make trade-offs between sound quality and file size. We can record and save the sound either in very high quality, leading to large files, or in lower quality, leading to smaller files. The settings we can vary are mainly

■ The sample format (usually 16-bit, 24-bit, or 32-bit).

■ The sample rate, measured in Hertz (Hz), varying usually from around 8,000 Hz to 96,000 Hz.

■ Stereo versus mono recording. (Stereo records two separate tracks, and thus produces twice the amount of data.)

If you look carefully at Figure 8.1, you can see that the sound in that screenshot was recorded in 32 bit, 44,100 Hz, stereo.

This is a typical default setting for sound recording programs, but actually much higher quality than what is needed for simple sound effects. (We might want this quality for listening to music that we like, but we don't need it for a short *Bang!* sound effect.)

In general, you should consider saving your sounds in lower quality, unless you feel you really need more quality.

**Exercise 8.20** Search your sound recording program for settings for sample format, sample rate, and stereo/mono recording. In some programs, you can convert existing sounds. In other programs, you can specify these settings only for new recordings. Make a sound recording with different sample formats, with different sample rates, and in stereo and mono. Save these as different files and compare the file sizes. Which change has the largest benefit for the file size?

**Exercise 8.21** Listen to the sounds produced in the previous exercise. Can you hear a difference? How much can you reduce the quality (and the file size) while still achieving acceptable quality?

## 8.5 Working with images

As discussed briefly in previous chapters (e.g., when we produced the asteroids background in Chapter 7), managing images for actors and world backgrounds can be achieved in two different ways: We can use prepared images from files, or we can draw an image on the fly in our program.

We shall discuss both methods in a little more detail here.

## 8.6 Image files and file formats

There are various ways to acquire images for our scenarios. The easiest is, of course, to use images from the Greenfoot image library. These are presented automatically when we create new classes. There are also several good libraries of free icons and images available on the Internet. A few minutes of searching should turn some of them up. (Make sure, however, that the images you want to use are really meant for free public use—not everything is free or in the public domain just because it is on the Internet. Respect other people's copyright and license terms.)

The most interesting alternative, however, if we want to make our scenarios unique and give them their own atmosphere, is to make images ourselves.

There are several graphics programs available that we can use to produce images. *Photoshop* is maybe the best known commercial program, and is certainly a very good one to use if you happen to have it. However, there are also free and open source programs that provide similar functionality. *Gimp*[2] is an excellent free program with many sophisticated features, and it is worth installing. There are also many simpler paint programs that could be used.

Producing good looking graphics takes some time to learn, and cannot be discussed in detail in this book. Play and practice, and you will figure out many techniques and tricks. Here, we shall concentrate on the technicalities of using the images.

---

[2] http://www.gimp.org

One of the important questions is what file formats to use when saving images. As with sounds, there is a trade-off to be made between quality and file size. Image files have the potential to be very large (much larger than the code files in our scenarios), so they can easily dominate the overall download size of our project. Again, this is particularly important if we want to export our scenario to a web server, such as the Greenfoot Gallery. Different image formats can lead to different file sizes by a factor of 10 or more, meaning that the scenario will download 10 times as fast (because it is only a tenth of the size) if we choose formats well.

Greenfoot can read images in JPEG, PNG, GIF, BMP, and TIFF formats. Of these, JPEG and PNG are the two best formats for most uses.

**Concept:**

The **JPEG** image format compresses large images very well. This is often the best choice for backgrounds.

JPEG images have the advantage that they compress very well. This means that they can be saved with very small file sizes. This is particularly true for full color images, such as photos and backgrounds (which is why many digital cameras use this format). When saving JPEG images, many graphics programs allow us to choose how much we want to compress the file. The more we compress, the smaller the file gets, but also quality is reduced. Gimp, for example, presents a "Quality" slider when we save an image in JPEG format. Reducing the quality creates smaller files.

**Exercise 8.22** Create an image in your graphics program and save it as a JPEG file. Save it with at least four different quality settings. Then open the different files and view them side by side. Also compare the file sizes. Which quality setting is a good compromise between picture quality and file size for your image?

**Exercise 8.23** In your graphics program, make a new background for your scenario that you created for the earlier sections of this chapter. Save it as a JPEG file. Use it in your scenario. Which size (height and width) should the image be? What happens if it is too big? What happens if it is too small?

**Exercise 8.24** How do you think the JPEG algorithm manages to make files smaller? How could this work? Try to come up with a few theories and guesses as to how this could be done.

**Exercise 8.25** How does JPEG actually compress files? Do some research on the Internet to find out and answer in writing.

**Concept:**

Pixels in images have a **transparency** value that determines whether we can see through them. Pixels may be partly transparent. If they are fully transparent, they are invisible.

**Concept:**

The **PNG** image format is often the best choice for actor images, since it can handle transparency and compresses fairly well.

The second image format that is very useful to us is PNG.

PNG images have the advantage that they can handle transparency very well. Any individual pixel can be partly or completely transparent. This allows us to create non-rectangular images. (As discussed in Chapter 7, all images are rectangular, but having transparent parts creates the appearance of arbitrary shapes.)

This ability to handle transparency, combined with good compression, makes PNG an ideal format for actor images. (JPEG images cannot have transparent pixels, so they cannot be used here, unless the actor happens to be rectangular. For backgrounds, this is generally not a problem, because we do not usually have transparency in backgrounds.)

There is rarely a need to use BMP, TIFF, or GIF images. BMP does not compress as well as other formats and does not support transparent pixels. TIFF images can preserve quality very well, but create larger file sizes. GIF is a proprietary format that has effectively been replaced by the better—and free—PNG format.

**Exercise 8.26** Make two new images for your actor (the actor will switch between these two images). Save them in PNG format. Make one of these images the default image for your actor class.

**Exercise 8.27** Modify your actor code so that it toggles between your two images every time the actor is clicked with the mouse.

**Exercise 8.28** Modify your actor code again so that it displays the second actor image only while the mouse is pressed. In other words, the actor starts off with a default image; when the mouse is pressed on the actor, it displays a different image, and as soon as the mouse is released, it reverts to its original image.

## 8.7 Drawing images

The second method to obtain images for our actors and backgrounds is to draw them programmatically. We have seen examples of this in some of the scenarios in earlier chapters, for example, when we painted the stars in the asteroids program.

Every pixel in an image is defined by two values: its color value and its transparency value (also called the *alpha value*).

The color value is again split into three components: the red, green, and blue component.[3] Colors represented this way are usually referred to as RGB colors.

This means that we can represent a pixel (with color and transparency) in four numbers. The order usually is as follows:

```
( R, G, B, A )
```

That is, the first three values define the red, green, and blue components (in this order), and the last is the alpha value.

In Java, all of these values are in the range [0..255] (zero to 255 inclusive). A color component value of 0 indicates no color in this component, while 255 is full strength. An alpha value of 0 is fully transparent (invisible), while 255 is opaque (solid).

Figure 8.2 shows a table of some of the possible colors, all with no transparency (alpha = 255). The table in Figure 8.2 was produced with the Greenfoot scenario *color-chart*, which is in the *chapter08* folder in the book scenarios.

---

[3] This is just one possible model to represent color. There are others in use in computer graphics and in print. However, this is the one most commonly used in Java programming, so we shall concentrate on this model here.

**Figure 8.2**
RGB color table

| | | | | | |
|---|---|---|---|---|---|
| 0,0,0 | 0,0,51 | 0,0,102 | 0,0,153 | 0,0,204 | 0,0,255 |
| 0,51,0 | 0,51,51 | 0,51,102 | 0,51,153 | 0,51,204 | 0,51,255 |
| 0,102,0 | 0,102,51 | 0,102,102 | 0,102,153 | 0,102,204 | 0,102,255 |
| 0,153,0 | 0,153,51 | 0,153,102 | 0,153,153 | 0,153,204 | 0,153,255 |
| 0,204,0 | 0,204,51 | 0,204,102 | 0,204,153 | 0,204,204 | 0,204,255 |
| 0,255,0 | 0,255,51 | 0,255,102 | 0,255,153 | 0,255,204 | 0,255,255 |
| 51,0,0 | 51,0,51 | 51,0,102 | 51,0,153 | 51,0,204 | 51,0,255 |
| 51,51,0 | 51,51,51 | 51,51,102 | 51,51,153 | 51,51,204 | 51,51,255 |
| 51,102,0 | 51,102,51 | 51,102,102 | 51,102,153 | 51,102,204 | 51,102,255 |
| 51,153,0 | 51,153,51 | 51,153,102 | 51,153,153 | 51,153,204 | 51,153,255 |
| 51,204,0 | 51,204,51 | 51,204,102 | 51,204,153 | 51,204,204 | 51,204,255 |
| 51,255,0 | 51,255,51 | 51,255,102 | 51,255,153 | 51,255,204 | 51,255,255 |
| 102,0,0 | 102,0,51 | 102,0,102 | 102,0,153 | 102,0,204 | 102,0,255 |
| 102,51,0 | 102,51,51 | 102,51,102 | 102,51,153 | 102,51,204 | 102,51,255 |
| 102,102,0 | 102,102,51 | 102,102,102 | 102,102,153 | 102,102,204 | 102,102,255 |
| 102,153,0 | 102,153,51 | 102,153,102 | 102,153,153 | 102,153,204 | 102,153,255 |
| 102,204,0 | 102,204,51 | 102,204,102 | 102,204,153 | 102,204,204 | 102,204,255 |
| 102,255,0 | 102,255,51 | 102,255,102 | 102,255,153 | 102,255,204 | 102,255,255 |
| 153,0,0 | 153,0,51 | 153,0,102 | 153,0,153 | 153,0,204 | 153,0,255 |
| 153,51,0 | 153,51,51 | 153,51,102 | 153,51,153 | 153,51,204 | 153,51,255 |
| 153,102,0 | 153,102,51 | 153,102,102 | 153,102,153 | 153,102,204 | 153,102,255 |
| 153,153,0 | 153,153,51 | 153,153,102 | 153,153,153 | 153,153,204 | 153,153,255 |
| 153,204,0 | 153,204,51 | 153,204,102 | 153,204,153 | 153,204,204 | 153,204,255 |
| 153,255,0 | 153,255,51 | 153,255,102 | 153,255,153 | 153,255,204 | 153,255,255 |
| 204,0,0 | 204,0,51 | 204,0,102 | 204,0,153 | 204,0,204 | 204,0,255 |
| 204,51,0 | 204,51,51 | 204,51,102 | 204,51,153 | 204,51,204 | 204,51,255 |
| 204,102,0 | 204,102,51 | 204,102,102 | 204,102,153 | 204,102,204 | 204,102,255 |
| 204,153,0 | 204,153,51 | 204,153,102 | 204,153,153 | 204,153,204 | 204,153,255 |
| 204,204,0 | 204,204,51 | 204,204,102 | 204,204,153 | 204,204,204 | 204,204,255 |
| 204,255,0 | 204,255,51 | 204,255,102 | 204,255,153 | 204,255,204 | 204,255,255 |
| 255,0,0 | 255,0,51 | 255,0,102 | 255,0,153 | 255,0,204 | 255,0,255 |
| 255,51,0 | 255,51,51 | 255,51,102 | 255,51,153 | 255,51,204 | 255,51,255 |
| 255,102,0 | 255,102,51 | 255,102,102 | 255,102,153 | 255,102,204 | 255,102,255 |
| 255,153,0 | 255,153,51 | 255,153,102 | 255,153,153 | 255,153,204 | 255,153,255 |
| 255,204,0 | 255,204,51 | 255,204,102 | 255,204,153 | 255,204,204 | 255,204,255 |
| 255,255,0 | 255,255,51 | 255,255,102 | 255,255,153 | 255,255,204 | 255,255,255 |

**Exercise 8.29** What do pixels look like which have a color/alpha value of (255, 0, 0, 255)? What about (0, 0, 255, 128)? And what is (255, 0, 255, 230)?

In Greenfoot, colors are represented by objects of the Color class from the java.awt package. After importing that class, we can create color objects either with just RGB values:

```
Color mycol = new Color (255, 12, 34);
```

or with RGB values and an alpha value:

```
Color mycol = new Color (255, 12, 34, 128);
```

If we do not specify an alpha value, the color will be fully opaque.

**Exercise 8.30** Create a new Greenfoot scenario called *color-test*. In it, create a world with a background that displays a pattern. Create an Actor subclass called ColorPatch. Program the ColorPatch class so that it generates a new GreenfootImage of a fixed size, filled with a fixed color. Use this image as the actor's image. Experiment with different color and alpha values.

**Exercise 8.31** Modify your code so that the color patch, when created, gets an image of a random size, filled with a random color, and random transparency.

**Exercise 8.32** Modify your code again so that the image is not filled, but instead has 100 small colored dots painted into it, at random locations within the actor's image.

## 8.8 Combining images files and dynamic drawing

Some of the most interesting visual effects are achieved when we combine static images from files with dynamic changes made by our program. We can, for example, start with a static image file, and then paint onto it with different colors, or scale it up or down, or let it fade by changing its transparency.

To try this out, we shall create a smoke effect. In our next scenario, we make a ball move across the screen, leaving a trail of smoke behind (see Figure 8.3).

**Exercise 8.33** Create a new scenario called *smoke*. Make a nice looking, fairly neutral background image for it.

**Exercise 8.34** Create a ball that moves across the screen at constant speed. When it hits the edge of the screen, it bounces off. (The screen is, in effect, a box, and the ball bounces within it.)

**Figure 8.3**
The smoke trail effect

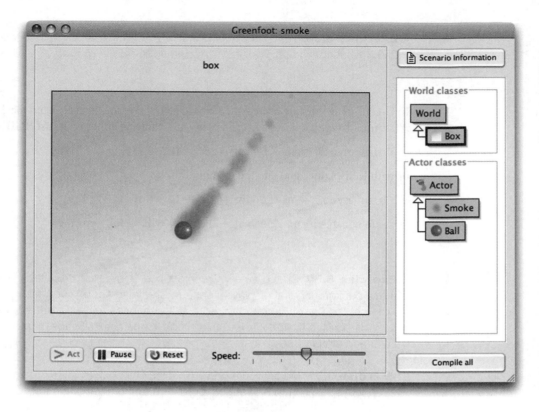

Now we shall work on the smoke effect. First, create an image showing a puff of smoke (Figure 8.4).

**Figure 8.4**
An image of a puff
of smoke

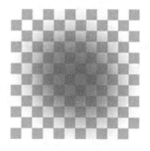

Note that the checkered background is not part of the image—it is shown here only to demonstrate that the smoke puff image is semi-transparent (we can see the background behind it).

Your smoke does not have to be green—you can make it any color you like—but it should be transparent. You can achieve this in a good graphics program by simply drawing a dot with a large, soft, semi-transparent paint brush. If you have trouble producing this image, you can use the prepared image file *smoke.png* from the *chapter08* folder in the book scenarios.

**Exercise 8.35** Create the smoke image as described above.

**Exercise 8.36** Create a `Smoke` actor class in your scenario. When inserted into the world, a smoke actor should fairly quickly fade away. That is, in every act cycle, the image of the actor should become smaller and more transparent. (The `GreenfootImage` class has methods to adjust the size and transparency.) When they are fully transparent or very small, they should remove themselves from the world.

**Exercise 8.37** Modify your ball so that it leaves puffs of smoke behind. Producing a puff of smoke every time the ball moves may be a little too much: Try creating a new smoke puff only in every second step of the ball. Test.

**Exercise 8.38** Modify your smoke so that it does not always fade at exactly the same rate. Make the rate of fading somewhat random, so that some puffs of smoke fade away more quickly than others.

If you completed all the exercises above, then you should now have a good looking smoke trail behind your ball. If you had trouble with these exercises, or if you want to compare your solution to ours, you can have a look at the smoke scenario in the book projects. This implements the task described here.

## 8.9 Summary

Being able to produce sounds and images is a very valuable skill for producing good looking games, simulations, and other graphical applications. Knowing about sound and image file formats is important to make good choices about trade-offs between file size and quality.

Sounds can be recorded and edited with a variety of sound recording programs, and various parameters determine the sound quality and file size. For Greenfoot scenarios, we usually use WAV format with fairly low quality.

Images can also be saved in a variety of different formats. Different formats vary in how well they compress files, how well they preserve image quality, and how they handle transparency. JPEG and PNG are the formats most often used for Greenfoot scenarios.

By combining images from a file with dynamic image operations, such as scaling and transparency changes, we can achieve attractive visual effects in our scenarios.

### Concept summary

- Sounds can be saved in a variety of different **formats** and **encodings**. Not all programs can play all sound formats. For Greenfoot, we usually use **WAV** format.

- The **sample format**, **sample rate**, and **stereo/mono** setting of a sound recording determine file size and sound quality.

■ The **JPEG** image format compresses large images very well. This is often the best choice for backgrounds.

■ Pixels in images have a **transparency** value that determines whether we can see through them. Pixels may be partly transparent. If they are fully transparent, they are invisible.

■ The **PNG** image format is often the best choice for actor images, since it can handle transparency and compresses fairly well.

# CHAPTER 9

# Simulations

topics:     simulations

concepts:   emergent behavior, experimentation

In this chapter, we shall discuss one type of software application in a little more detail: simulations.

Simulations are fascinating examples of computing, because they are highly experimental, and potentially allow us to predict the future. Many types of simulations can be (and have been) developed for computers: traffic simulations, weather forecasting systems, economics simulations (simulations of stock markets), simulations of chemical reactions, nuclear explosions, environmental simulations, and many more.

We have seen one simple simulation in Chapter 6, in which we simulated part of a solar system. That simulation was a little too simplistic to accurately forecast trajectories of real planets, but there are some aspects of astrophysics that that simulation may help us understand.

In general, simulations may serve two different purposes: they can be used to study and understand the system they are simulating, or they can be used for forecasting.

In the first case, the modeling of a system (such as the modeling of the stars and planets) may help us understand some aspects of how it behaves. In the second case, if we have an accurate simulation, we can play through "what if" scenarios. For example, we might have a traffic simulation for a city, and we observe that every morning a traffic jam develops at a certain intersection in the real city. How can we improve the situation? Should we build a new roundabout? Or change the traffic light signal patterns? Or maybe we should build a bypass?

The effects of any of these interventions are often hard to predict. We cannot try out all these options in real life to see which is best, since that would be too disruptive and expensive. But we can simulate them. In our traffic simulation, we can try out each option and see how it improves traffic.

If the simulation is accurate, then the result we observe in the simulation will also be true in real life. But this is a big "if": Developing a simulation that is accurate enough is not easy, and it is a lot of work. But for many systems, it is possible to a useful degree.

Weather forecasting simulations are now accurate enough that a one-day forecast is fairly reliable. A seven-day forecast, however, is about as good as rolling dice: The simulations are just not good enough.

**Concept:**

A **simulation** is a computer program that simulates some phenomena from the real world. If simulations are accurate enough, we can learn interesting things about the real world from observing them.

When we use simulations, it is important to be aware of the limitations: Firstly, simulations always have a degree of inaccuracy because we are not modeling the behaviors of the actors completely realistically and because we may not know the exact state of the starting system.

In addition, simulations necessarily model only part of reality, and we must be aware that parts outside of our simulation might actually be relevant.

In the example of our traffic jam, for instance, maybe the best solution is neither of the options mentioned above, but to provide better public transport or bicycle lanes to get some cars off the road. If our simulation does not include that aspect, we would never find out just by using the simulation, no matter how accurate it is.

Despite these limitations, however, good simulations are incredibly useful, and even very simple simulations are fascinating to play with. They are so useful, in fact, that almost all of the world's fastest computers run simulations most of the time, or at least a substantial part of their time.

---

**Side note: Supercomputers**

A list of the fastest supercomputers in the world is regularly published on the Internet at http://www.top500.org. Most of these are described there in some detail, and for many of them, the list includes links to web sites that describe their purpose and the kind of work they are used for.

Reading through this material, you can see that many are run by large research institutions or the military and that almost all are used to run simulations, often physics simulations. The military use these, for example, to test nuclear explosions in simulations, and research institutions conduct many different science experiments this way.

---

Simulations also have a special place in the history of object-oriented programming: Object orientation was invented explicitly to run simulations.

The very first object-oriented programming language, named *Simula*, was designed in the 1960s by Kristen Nygaard and Ole-Johan Dahl at the Norwegian Computer Center in Oslo. As the name suggests, its purpose was to build simulations. All object-oriented programming languages today can be traced back to that language. Dahl and Nygaard received the 2001 Turing Award—computer science's equivalent of the Nobel prize—for this work.

Enough introduction—let's get our hands on the keyboard again and try out some things.

In this chapter, we shall look at one simulation fairly briefly and then work on writing another one in more detail.

## 9.1 Foxes and rabbits

The first simulation we investigate is called *foxes-and-rabbits*. It is a typical example of a class of simulations called *predator-prey-simulations*—a type of simulation in which one creature chases (and eats) another. In our case, the predator is a fox and the prey is a rabbit.

The idea here is as follows: The scenario shows a field that contains populations of foxes and rabbits. Foxes are represented by blue squares, and rabbits are shown as yellow squares.

**Figure 9.1**

The foxes-and-rabbits simulation

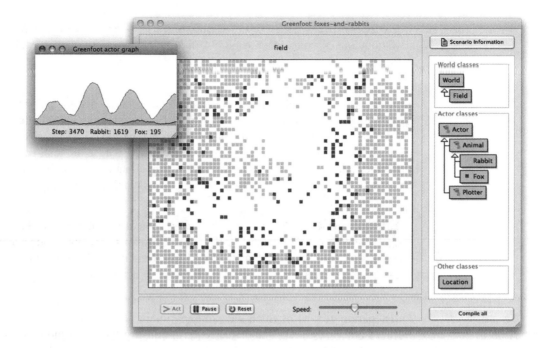

Both species have fairly simple behavior: Rabbits move around and—if they are old enough—may produce offspring. There is a set probability at each act step for rabbits to reproduce. There are two ways in which rabbits may die: They may die of old age, or they may be eaten by a fox.

Foxes move and breed in a manner similar to rabbits (although they breed less frequently and have fewer young). One additional thing, however, that they do is hunt. If they are hungry, and they see a rabbit sitting next to them, they will move to eat the rabbit.

Foxes can also die in two different ways: They can die of old age, and they can starve. If they do not find a rabbit to eat for some time, they will die. (Rabbits are assumed to always find sufficient amounts of food.)

> **Exercise 9.1** Open the *foxes-and-rabbits* scenario. Run it. Explain the patterns of populations and movement you see emerging in the field.
>
> **Exercise 9.2** You will notice that this scenario shows a second small window with a population graph. One curve shows the number of foxes, the other the number of rabbits. Explain the shape of these graphs.

As we can see, the simulation is highly simplistic in many ways: Animals do not have to meet mates to reproduce (they can do that all on their own), food sources for rabbits are not included in the simulation, other factors of death (such as diseases) are ignored, and many factors are left out. However, the parameters that we do simulate are already fairly interesting, and we can do some experiments with them.

> **Exercise 9.3** Are the current populations stable? That is, does it always continue to run without one of the species dying out? If species become extinct, what is the average time they survive?

Does the size of the field matter? For example, imagine we have a national park with an endangered species. And someone wants to build a freeway through the middle of it that the animals cannot cross, essentially dividing the park into two parks of half the size each. The proponents of the freeway might argue that this does not matter because the total size of parkland is about the same as before. The park authority might argue that this is bad because it halves the size of each park. Who is right? Does the size of a park matter? Do some experiments.

> **Exercise 9.4** The `Field` class has definitions of constants toward the top of its source code for its width and height. Modify these constants to change the size of the field. Does the size of the field affect the stability of the populations? Do species die out more easily if the field is smaller or larger? Or does it make no difference?

Other parameters with which we can experiment are defined in constants at the top of the `Rabbit` and `Fox` classes. Rabbits have definitions for their maximum age, the age from which they can breed, the frequency of breeding (defined as a probability for each step), and the maximum size of their litter when they do breed. Foxes have the same parameters and an additional one: the nutritional value of a rabbit when it is eaten (expressed as the number of steps that the fox can survive after eating the rabbit). The food level of a fox decreases by one in every step and increases when eating a rabbit. If it ever reaches zero, the fox dies.

> **Exercise 9.5** Choose a field size in which the populations are almost stable but occasionally die out. Then make changes to the `Rabbit` parameters to try to increase the chances of the populations' survival. Can you find settings that make the populations more stable? Do some settings make them less stable? Are the observed effects as you expected, or did some differ from your expectations?

> **Exercise 9.6** When the fox population is in danger of becoming extinct occasionally, we could speculate that we could improve the chances of foxes' survival by increasing the food value of rabbits. If foxes can live longer on eating a single rabbit, they should starve less often. Investigate this hypothesis. Double the amount of the `RABBIT_FOOD_VALUE` constant and test. Does the fox population survive longer? Explain the result.

> **Exercise 9.7** Make other changes to the `Fox` parameters. Can you make the populations more stable?

The exercises show that we can experiment with this simulation by changing some parameters and observing their effects. In this chapter, however, we shall not be content with experimenting with an existing simulation, we also want to develop our own.

We shall do that in the next section with a different scenario: *ants*.

## 9.2 Ants

The *ants* scenario simulates the food collecting behavior of ant colonies. Or, to be more precise, we would like it to simulate this behavior, but it does not do it yet. We shall develop it to do so. In its current state, the scenario has been prepared to some extent: The graphics exist and some of the implementation has been completed. The main functionality, however, is missing, and we shall work on completing it.

> **Exercise 9.8** Open the scenario called *ants* from the *chapter09* folder of the book scenarios. Create an ant hill in the world and run the scenario. What do you observe?
>
> **Exercise 9.9** Examine the source code of the Ant class. What does it currently do?
>
> **Exercise 9.10** Ant is a subclass of class `Creature`. What functionality does a creature have?

**Figure 9.2**

The ants simulation

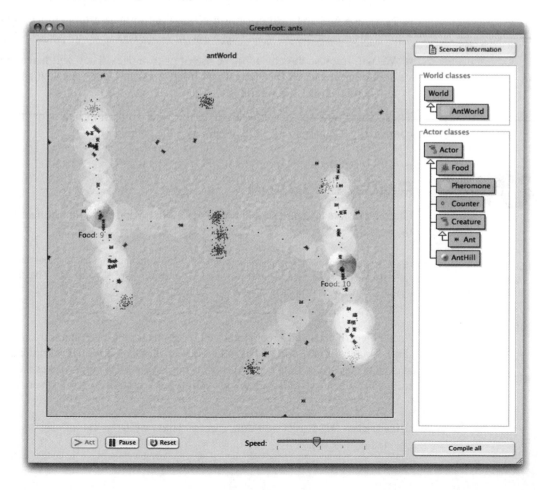

> **Exercise 9.11** Examine the source code of class `AntHill`. What does this class do? How many ants are in an ant hill?

The first thing we notice is that the ants do not move. They are created in the middle of the ant hill, but since they do not move, after a short while they will all sit there on top of each other. So the first thing for us to do is to make ants move.

> **Exercise 9.12** In the `Ant`'s `act` method, add a line of code to make the ant move. Consult the documentation of class `Creature` to find out about the methods to use.

We shall now go step by step through a series of improvements to this scenario. The steps we shall take are as follows:

- We will introduce some food to the scenario, so that the ants have something to collect.

- We will improve the ants, so that they can find the food and carry some of it home.

- Next, we will add a `Pheromone` class. Pheromones are chemical substances that some animals produce to leave messages for other animals of their species.

- We will improve the ants to make use of pheromones: They will leave drops of pheromones on the ground when they have found food, and other ants can then smell these pheromones and adjust where they are going.

These steps together roughly simulate the food collecting behavior of ant colonies. When complete, we can do some experiments with the simulation.

## 9.3 Collecting food

Our first task is to create some food in our scenario and to let ants collect it and carry it back to the ant hill.

> **Exercise 9.13** Create a new class called **Food**. The class does not need a fixed image. We will draw the image from within the class.

Each object of class **Food** represents a pile of food crumbs. Our plan is to create a new, dynamically drawn image for the **Food** object and draw a small dot on it for every crumb in the pile. A pile may start with, say, 100 crumbs, and every time an ant finds the pile, it takes a few crumbs away. That means that the image must be redrawn with fewer crumbs every time an ant takes some food.

> **Exercise 9.14** In class **Food**, create a field for the number of crumbs currently in the pile. Initialize it to 100.

**Exercise 9.15** Create a new private method called `updateImage`, which creates an image of a fixed size and draws a dot on it at a random location for each crumb currently in the pile. Choose a size for the image of the pile that you think looks good. Call this method from the constructor.

If you completed the exercise above, and you placed food crumbs at a random location within the `Food` image (using the `Greenfoot.getRandomNumber` method to obtain the coordinates), then you will notice that the pile of crumbs has a somewhat square-ish shape (Figure 9.3a). This is because the image itself is square, and the crumbs are evenly distributed over the image.

If we want to change this to look more like a pile (with most crumbs toward the middle, and other crumbs in a rough circle-shape around it, Figure 9.3b), then we can use another random number method to place the crumbs differently. We shall do this with exercises 9.16 and 9.17. Note that these are more advanced exercises and they are purely cosmetic: They merely change the look of the food pile, and none of its functionality, so they could safely be skipped.

**Exercise 9.16** Consult the API documentation for the standard Java class library. Find the documentation for class **Random** from the `java.util` package. Objects of this class are *random number generators* that are more flexible than Greenfoot's `getRandomNumber` method. The method of interest to us is the one that returns random numbers in a Gaussian distribution (also called a "normal distribution"). What is the method's name, and what does it do?

**Exercise 9.17** In your **Food** class, change your placement of food crumbs in the image to make use of the Gaussian distribution of random numbers. For this, you have to use a `java.util.Random` object to create the random numbers, instead of `Greenfoot.getRandomNumber`.

**Figure 9.3**
Placement of food crumbs with different randomizer algorithms

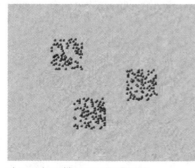

a) crumbs with even distribution

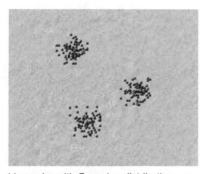

b) crumbs with Gaussian distribution

> **Side note: Random distributions**
>
> If we need random behavior in our programs, it is sometimes important to think about what kind of random distribution we need. Many random functions, such as the `Greenfoot.getRandomNumber` method, produce a *uniform distribution*. In this, the chance of every possible result occurring is the same. The Gaussian random number function gives us a *normal distribution*. This is one in which the average results are more likely to occur, and more extreme results are rarer.
>
> If we, for example, program a dice game, we need a uniform distribution. Each side of the die is evenly likely to come up. On the other hand, if we model the speed of cars in a traffic simulation, a normal distribution would be better. Most cars are driving somewhere close to the average speed, and only few cars are very slow or very fast.

Next, we need to add functionality to remove some crumbs from the food pile, so that ants can take some food.

> **Exercise 9.18** Add a public method to class **Food** that removes a few crumbs from the pile. Make sure that the image is redrawn with the correct number of remaining crumbs. When the crumbs are all gone, the **Food** object should remove itself from the world. Test this method interactively.

Now that we have a pile of food available in our scenario, we shall make our ants collect it. Ants will now switch between two different behaviors:

■ If they are not carrying food, they search for food.

■ If they are currently carrying food, they walk toward home.

Ants switch between these two behaviors when they reach either a food pile or the home ant hill. If they are searching for food, and they run into a food pile, they pick up some food and switch from the first to the second behavior. If they then reach the ant hill, they drop the food there and switch back to the first behavior pattern.

We shall now implement this in our `Ant` class. Written in pseudo code, the `act` method might look somewhat like this:

```
if (carrying food) {
    walk towards home;
    check whether we are home;
}
else {
    search for food;
}
```

We implement this now one step at a time.

**Exercise 9.19** In the `Ant` class, implement a `searchForFood` method. This method should initially just do a random walk and check whether we have run into a food pile. If we find a food pile, stop execution. (This is just to test whether we have correctly detected the food.)

**Exercise 9.20** Add functionality to pick up some food when we find a food pile (instead of stopping execution). We need to remove some crumbs from the food pile (we should already have a method for this), note that we are now carrying food (we probably need a field for this), and change the ant's image. There is already an image prepared in the scenario, named *ant-with-food.png*, that you can use.

**Exercise 9.21** Ensure that the ant walks toward home when carrying food.

**Exercise 9.22** Implement a method that checks whether an ant has reached the home hill. If it has reached home, it should drop its food. Dropping the food consists of noting that it is not carrying food anymore (including changing the image back) and calling the `AntHill`'s `countFood` method to record that it has collected this food crumb.

**Concept:**

Using **short methods** with a specific purpose leads to better **code quality**.

Pay attention to the quality of your code: Use short methods with distinct purposes and make sure to comment your methods well. Do not write too much code into a single method.

You can find an implementation of the functionality discussed so far in the scenario *ants-2*. After completing your implementation (or when you get stuck), you might like to compare your solution with ours.

## 9.4 Setting up the world

Before we go on to add pheromones to our scenario, let us first add some initialization code that creates some ant hills and food for us automatically, so that we do not have to repeat this manually every time we wish to test.

**Exercise 9.23** Add code to class `AntWorld`, so that it automatically creates two ant hills and a few piles of food in the world.

## 9.5 Adding pheromones

Now that we have a good start setup, we are ready to add pheromones. Each pheromone object is a small drop of a chemical substance that the ants leave on the ground. This drop will evaporate fairly quickly and then disappear.

Ants drop pheromones while they are walking back home from a food source. When other ants smell the drop of pheromone, they can then turn away from their home hill and walk in the direction toward the food.

**Exercise 9.24** Create a class `Pheromone`. This class does not need an image—we shall draw the image programmatically.

**Exercise 9.25** Implement an `updateImage` method in the `Pheromone` class. Initially, this method should create an image with a white circle drawn onto it and set this as the actor's image. The white circle should be partly transparent. Call this method from the constructor.

**Exercise 9.26** Give the pheromones an *intensity* attribute. (That is, add an `intensity` field.) The intensity of a pheromone object should start out at a defined maximum intensity, and decrease in every act cycle. When the intensity reaches 0, remove the pheromone object from the world. A drop of pheromone should evaporate in about 180 act cycles.

**Exercise 9.27** Modify your `updateImage` method, so that it makes use of the pheromone's intensity. As the intensity decreases, the white circle representing it on screen should become smaller and more transparent. Make sure `updateImage` is called from the `act` method so that we see the image change on screen.

**Exercise 9.28** Test your pheromones by placing them into the world manually and running your simulation.

We now have a `Pheromone` class available that our ants can use. Now we only have to get the ants to use it. The first half of using the pheromone is placing it into the world. (The second half is noticing it and changing direction as a result.) Let us do the first half first.

**Exercise 9.29** Add a method to your ant that places a drop of pheromone into the world. Call this method repeatedly while the ant is walking home.

If, in the previous exercise, you placed a drop of pheromone at every act cycle, you will notice that this places too much pheromone into the world. Ants cannot produce unlimited amounts of pheromones. After placing a drop, they need some time to regenerate more pheromone.

**Exercise 9.30** Modify the ant so that it can leave a drop of pheromone at most every 18 steps. To achieve this, you will need a field that stores the current pheromone level of an ant. When the ant places a pheromone drop, the pheromone level (remaining pheromones in the ant's body) goes down to 0, and then it slowly rises again until the ant is ready to leave another drop.

Figure 9.4 shows a trail of pheromones left by our ant at this point.[1] The drops are spaced out (the ant needs some time to regenerate pheromones), and the older pheromone drops are partly evaporated—they are smaller and more transparent.

**Figure 9.4**

An ant leaving a trail of pheromones

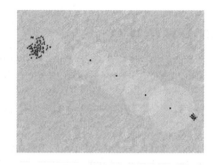

The final thing to add is for ants to smell the pheromones, and change their direction of movement when they do.

If an ant smells a drop of pheromone, it should walk away from its home hill for some limited time. If it does not find food or smell a new drop of pheromone after some time, then it should revert to random walking. Our algorithm for searching for food might look something like this:

```
if (we recently found a drop of pheromone) {
    walk away from home;
}
else if (we smell pheromone now) {
    walk towards the center of the pheromone drop;
    if (we are at the pheromone drop center) {
        note that we found pheromone;
    }
}
else {
    walk randomly;
}
check for food;
```

When implementing this in your own scenario, remember to create a separate method for each distinct subtask. That way, your code will remain well structured, easy to understand, and easy to modify.

**Exercise 9.31** Implement the functionality discussed above in your own scenario: When ants smell pheromones, they walk away from their home hill for the next 30 steps, before reverting to their default behavior.

---

[1] If you look closely, you will notice that I have modified my pheromone image to have a small dark dot in the middle. This is so that pheromones can be seen better even when they are quite transparent.

If you completed this exercise, then your ant simulation is more or less complete (as much as any software application is ever complete). If you run your scenario now, you should see ants forming paths to the food sources.

## 9.6 Path forming

**Concept:**

Simulations of systems often display **emergent behavior**. This is behavior not programmed into single actors, but emerging as a result of the sum of all behaviors.

One interesting aspect of this scenario is that there is no code anywhere in the project that talks about forming paths. The behavior of the individual ants is quite simple ("if you have food, go home; if you smell pheromones, go away; otherwise go anywhere"). However, together, the ants display some fairly sophisticated behavior: They form stable paths, refreshing the pheromones as they evaporate, and efficiently transport food back to their ant hill.

This is known as *emergent behavior*. It is behavior that is not programmed into any individual actor, but system behavior that emerges from the interactions of many (fairly simple) actors.

Most complex systems display some sort of emergent system behavior, whether they are traffic systems in cities, networks of computers, or crowds of people. Predicting these effects is very difficult, and computer simulations can help in understanding such systems.

**Exercise 9.32** How realistic is our simulation of the use of pheromones by ants? Do some research into the actual use of pheromones by ant colonies and write down which aspects of our simulation are realistic, and where we have made simplifications.

**Exercise 9.33** Assume pollution has introduced a toxic substance into the ants' environment. The effect is that their production of pheromones is reduced to a quarter of the previous amount. (The time between leaving drops of pheromones is four times as long.) Will they still be able to form paths? Test.

**Exercise 9.34** Assume another pollutant has decreased the ants' ability to remember that they recently smelled a pheromone to a third. Instead of 30 steps, they can only remember the pheromone for 10 steps. What is the effect of this on their behavior?

There are many more experiments you can do. The most obvious is to try out different placements of ant hills and food sources, and different values for the attributes that determine the ants' behavior.

The scenario *ants-3* in the *chapter09* folder shows an implementation of the tasks discussed above. It includes three different setup methods in the world class that can be called interactively from the antWorld popup menu.

## 9.7 Summary

In this chapter, we have seen two examples of simulations. This served two purposes. Firstly, this was a chance to practice many of the programming techniques we have discussed in earlier chapters, and we had to use most of the Java constructs previously introduced. Secondly, simulations are an interesting kind of application to experiment with. Many simulations are used in real life for many purposes, such as weather forecasting, traffic planning, environmental impact studies, physics research, and many more.

If you managed to solve all the exercises in this chapter, then you have understood a great deal of what this book tried to teach you, and you are competent with the basics of programming.

## Concept summary

- A **simulation** is a computer program that simulates some phenomena from the real world. If simulations are accurate enough, we can learn interesting things about the real world from observing them.

- Using **short methods** with a specific purpose leads to better **code quality**.

- Simulations of systems often display **emergent behavior**. This is behavior not programmed into single actors, but emerging as a result of the sum of all behaviors.

# Additional scenario ideas

| | |
|---|---|
| **topics:** | ideas for more scenarios |
| **concepts:** | (no new concepts introduced) |

This is the last chapter of this book. It is different from the other chapters in that it does not try to teach you any new concepts or techniques of programming. Instead it briefly presents a number of additional scenarios to give you some ideas for other things you might like to investigate and work on.

All scenarios presented here are also available as Greenfoot projects with source code in the book scenarios. However, most of them are not complete implementations of the idea they represent.

Some scenarios are almost complete, and you may like to study them to learn further techniques and see how certain effects were achieved. Others are beginnings, partial implementations of an idea which you could take as a starting point for your own project. Yet other ones are illustrations of a single concept or idea that might provide inspiration for something you could incorporate into one of your own scenarios.

In short, view these as a collection of ideas for future projects, and study them for a small glimpse into what else is possible for a competent programmer to achieve.

## 10.1 Marbles

The *marbles* scenario (Figure 10.1) implements a game in which you roll a golden ball over a board with the aim of clearing the board of all silver balls within a limited number of moves. The game is reasonably complete.

Several things are worth observing about this scenario. The first thing that stands out is that it looks quite nice. This has very little to do with Java or Greenfoot programming and is mostly due to the use of nice graphics. Using nicely designed graphics and sounds can make a big difference in the attractiveness of a game.

*Marbles* uses a nice looking background image (the game board and scroll for the text display) and actors with semi-transparent drop shadows (the marbles and the obstacles).

**Figure 10.1**
The Marbles game

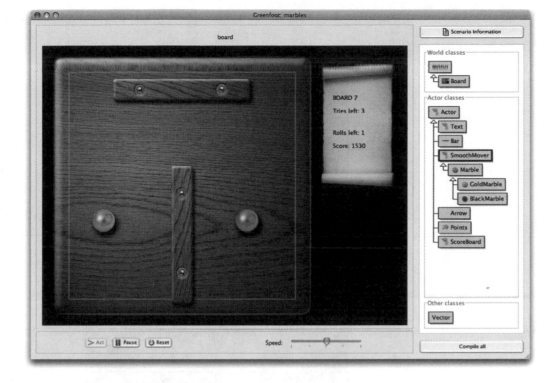

The other interesting aspect to examine is the collision detection. The marbles do not use any of the built-in Greenfoot collision detection methods, since these all work on the rectangular actor images. The marbles, on the other hand, are round, and we need precise collision for this.

Luckily, when the actors are round, this is not very difficult. Two marbles collide if their distance (measured from their center points) is less than their diameter. We know the diameter, and the distance is fairly easy to compute (using the Pythagoras theorem).

The next interesting thing is the way the new movement direction of a colliding marble is computed. There is a little trigonometry involved here, but if you are familiar with that, then it is not too hard.

Collisions with the fixed obstacles are easier, since they are always horizontally or vertically oriented rectangles. Therefore, a marble hitting one of these obstacles simply reverses its direction along one of the axes ($x$ or $y$).

You could reuse the marble collision logic for all sorts of other games that involve collision of round objects.

## 10.2 Lifts

The *lifts* scenario (Figure 10.2) shows a simple lift (or elevator) simulation. It shows several floors of a multistory building and three lifts moving up and down. People appear on the floors and press the call buttons and enter the lifts when they come.

**Figure 10.2**
A (partial) lift
simulation

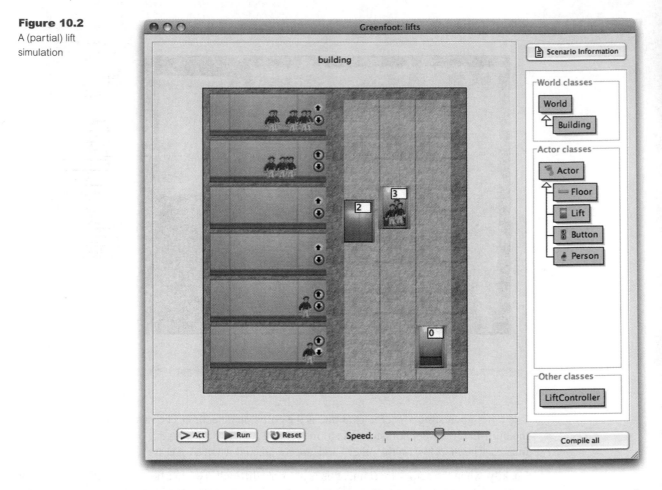

This is actually a very rudimentary, unfinished implementation. Much of what we see on the screen is fake: It does not properly simulate what is going on, and is just written for show effect.

For example, the people do not properly enter the lifts (they are just erased when a lift reaches a floor). The number of people shown in a lift is just a random number. Lifts also do not react to call buttons—they just move up and down randomly. There is no control algorithm implemented for the lifts.

So this is just a quick demo that presents the idea and the graphics. To finish the project, the movement of people would have to be properly modeled (in and out of the elevators). And then we could experiment with implementing and testing different lift control algorithms.

## 10.3 Boids

The *boids* example (Figure 10.3) shows a simulation of flocking behavior of birds.

The term "boids" comes from a program developed in 1986 by Craig Reynolds that first implemented this flocking algorithm. In it, each bird flies according to three rules:

**Figure 10.3**

Boids: A simulation
of flocking behavior

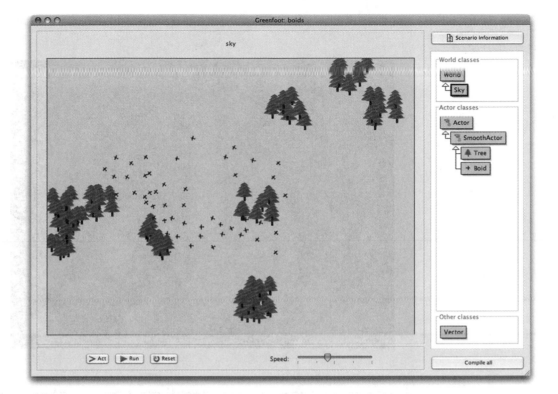

- Separation: steer away from other birds if getting too close.

- Alignment: steer toward the average heading of other birds in the vicinity.

- Cohesion: steer to move toward the average position of other birds in the vicinity.

With this algorithm, the birds develop movement that is quite nice to look at. Included in this scenario is also obstacle avoidance: trying not to fly into trees.

A version of this algorithm was used, for example, in Tim Burton's 1992 film "Batman Returns" to create animation for computer-generated swarms of bats and penguin flocks, and in the "Lord of the Rings" films to create the movement of the Orc armies.

The version for this book was written by Poul Henriksen.

You can find out much more about this by searching the web for "boids". And while this scenario currently does nothing other than show the movement, one feels that there has to be a game in it somewhere . . .

## 10.4    Circles

*Circles* (Figure 10.4) is a project that does not seem to have much of a purpose but is interesting to play with and nice to look at.

**Figure 10.4**
"Circles" is a mixture
of physics and art

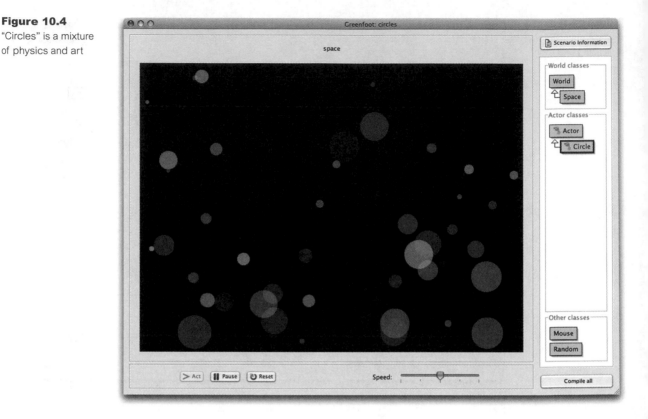

It uses some physical simulation, such as gravity and bouncing off edges, and some randomness to create beautiful moving images. Is it physics? Is it art? Or maybe a bit of both?

Whatever it is, I am sure there are many other ways to produce interesting or beautiful images, patterns, or color animations. (One idea might be to combine the circles with the collision detection algorithm from the Marbles game.)

*Circles* was written by Joe Lenton.

## 10.5 Explosion

The *explosion* scenario (Figure 10.5) demonstrates how we can implement a more spectacular looking explosion effect. The object that explodes is, in this case, a simple rock that we have encountered in other scenarios before. (It played, for example, the role of the asteroid in the *asteroids* scenario.) But we could really explode anything we like.

To achieve this effect, we have a `Debris` class that represents a part of the rock. When the rock explodes, we remove it from the world and place 40 pieces of debris in its place.

Each piece of debris is randomly stretched and rotated to make it look somewhat unique, and initially has a movement vector in a random direction. At every step, we add a bit of

**Figure 10.5**
An explosion effect

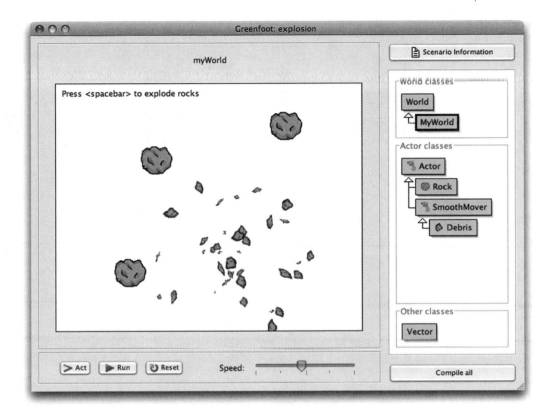

downward movement to simulate gravity, and the result is the explosion you see when you run this scenario.

A tutorial video explaining this scenario in more detail is available on the Greenfoot web site at `http://www.greenfoot.org/doc/videos.html`.

## 10.6 Breakout

"Breakout" (Figure 10.6) is a classic computer game in which the player controls a paddle at the bottom of the screen to bounce a ball upwards to remove some blocks. If you do not know the game, do a web search and you will quickly find out.

The *breakout* scenario is a partial implementation of this game. It uses the ball with the smoke effect that we discussed in Chapter 8 and adds a paddle for the player to control the ball. It has, however, no blocks to aim for, so in its current form it is not very interesting.

Many variations of breakout have been created over time. Many use different patterns of layout for the blocks at different levels. Most also have some "power-ups"—goodies hidden behind some blocks that float down when the block is removed. Catching them typically makes something interesting happen in the game (extra balls, increased speed, larger or smaller paddles, etc.)

Completing this game in an interesting way can make a good project. It could also be modified to have two paddles, one on either side, essentially turning it into the classic "Pong" game.

**Figure 10.6**
The beginning of a "breakout" game

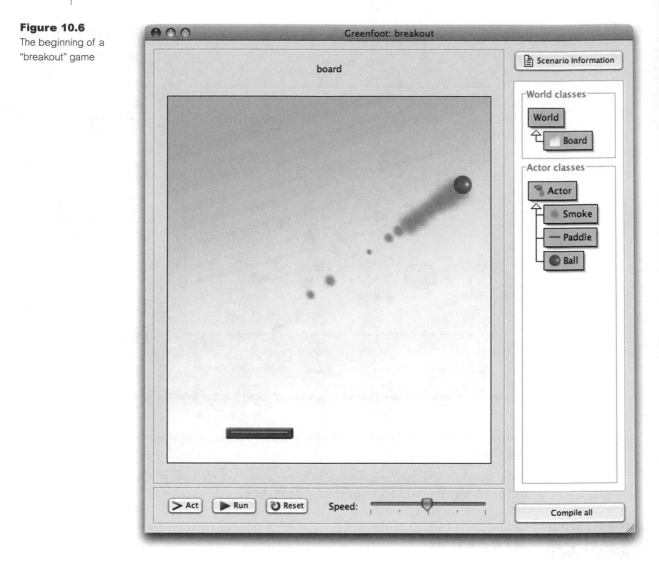

## 10.7 Platform jumper

A very common style of game is a "platform" game. The player typically controls a game character that has to move from one area on the screen to another, while overcoming various obstacles. One such obstacle may be a gap in the ground the character is walking on, with some means of getting across it.

The *pengu* scenario (Figure 10.7) implements a small segment of such a game. There are two pieces of ground on either side of the screen, and the penguin can get across by jumping onto a moving cloud.

This scenario is included here to demonstrate how an actor can move along the top of another (the penguin on top of the ground), and how jumping and falling might be implemented.

**Figure 10.7**

A start of a simple platform jumper game

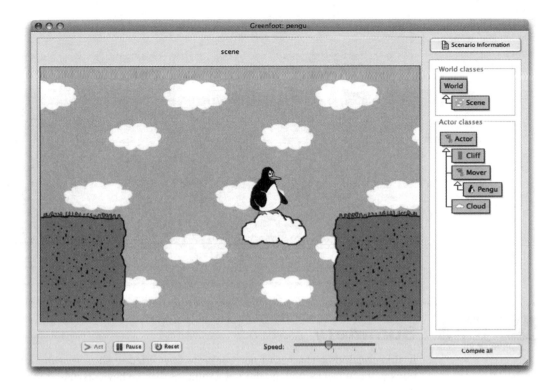

A tutorial video discussing this in more detail is available on the Greenfoot web site at http://www.greenfoot.org/doc/videos.html, under the name "Running, jumping and falling".

## 10.8 Wave

The last scenario presented here is called *wave* (Figure 10.8). It is a simple simulation of the propagation of a wave on a piece of string. Play around with it for a little while, and you will discover what it does.

One of the fascinating aspects of this example is how a fairly simple implementation—in each act round, each bead simply moves toward the middle of its two neighbors—achieves a quite sophisticated simulation of various aspects of wave propagation.

This example is included here to illustrate that, with a bit of thought and preparation, various behaviors from other disciplines could be simulated. In this case, it is a simple physical effect. Equally, one could simulate chemical reactions, biological interactions, interactions of sub-atomic particles, and much more. With some careful planning, we can learn something about other application areas, as well as learning about programming.

This scenario also implements slider and switch controls, which may be useful in other projects.

**Figure 10.8**
Simulation of wave
propagation on a
string of beads

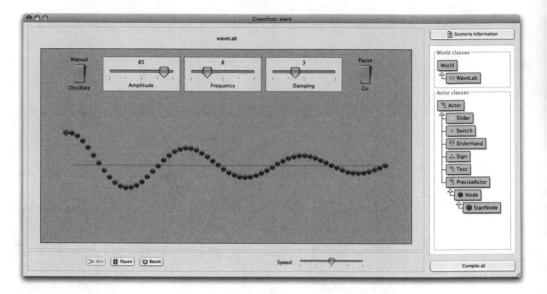

**Figure 10.8**
Simulation of wave
propagation on a
string of beads

## 10.9  Summary

In this concluding chapter of our book, we have tried to show that there are many more directions you can follow, beyond the few examples that we have discussed in more detail throughout this book.

As you become more experienced, you will become more confident and more able to turn your ideas into reality as you develop your programs. As a programmer, an infinite world of creative endeavor lies in front of you, both within Greenfoot and without, using other development environments.

When you program in other environments, outside of Greenfoot, you will have to learn new skills and techniques, but everything you have learned using Greenfoot will be useful and applicable.

If you have followed this book all the way through to this point, you have learned a great deal about programming in Java, and indeed programming in an object-oriented language in general. In learning to program, the beginning is always the hardest part, and you have that behind you.

If you would like support and ideas for further Greenfoot programming, make use of the Greenfoot web site.[1] Use the Greenfoot Gallery to publish your scenarios, look at other people's work, and get some ideas. Look at the video tutorials for tips and tricks. And join the discussion group to chat to other Greenfoot programmers, get and give help, and discuss new ideas.

We hope that you have come to enjoy programming as much as we do. If you have, a whole new world lies before you. Program, enjoy, and be creative!

---

[1] www.greenfoot.org

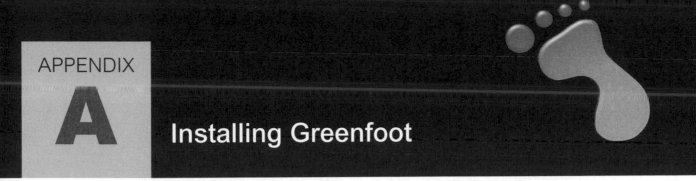

# Installing Greenfoot

This appendix will tell you where to find the Greenfoot software and the scenarios used with this book, and how to install them.

To work with the example projects in this book, you will need to install three things: A Java system, the Greenfoot software, and the book scenarios.

## A.1 Installing Java

Download Java from `http://java.sun.com/javase/downloads`. You should install the latest version of the Java SE Development Kit (JDK).

On Mac OS X, Java does not need to be installed—it is included in the standard Mac OS installation.

## A.2 Installing Greenfoot

Download Greenfoot from `http://www.greenfoot.org`, and follow the installation instructions.

## A.3 Installing the book scenarios

Download the book scenarios from `http://www.greenfoot.org/book`. You will receive a file named *book-scenarios.zip*. This is a compressed *zip* file that must be extracted. On Windows systems, this can usually be achieved by right-clicking and selecting *Extract All* from the menu. On Mac OS and Linux systems, you can double-click the file to extract it.

After extracting this file, you will have a folder named *book-scenarios* stored in your file system. Remember where you saved it—you will need to open the projects from this folder while you work through the book.

The Greenfoot API consists of five classes:

| | |
|---|---|
| Actor | Actor methods are available to all actor subclasses. |
| World | World methods are available to the world. |
| Greenfoot | Used to communicate with the Greenfoot environment itself. |
| MouseInfo | Provides information about the last mouse event. |
| GreenfootImage | For image presentation and manipulation. |

---

### Class World

| | |
|---|---|
| **World**(int worldWidth, int worldHeight, int cellSize) | Construct a new world. |
| void **act**() | Act method for the world. Called once per act round. |
| void **addObject**(Actor object, int x, int y) | Add an Actor to the world. |
| GreenfootImage **getBackground**() | Return the world's background image. |
| int **getCellSize**() | Return the size of a cell (in pixels). |
| Color **getColorAt**(int x, int y) | Return the color at the center of the cell. |
| int **getHeight**() | Return the height of the world (in number of cells). |
| List **getObjects**(Class cls) | Get all the objects in the world. |
| List **getObjectsAt**(int x, int y, Class cls) | Return all objects at a given cell. |
| int **getWidth**() | Return the width of the world (in number of cells). |
| int **numberOfObjects**() | Get the number of actors currently in the world. |
| void **removeObject**(Actor object) | Remove an object from the world. |
| void **removeObjects**(Collection objects) | Remove a list of objects from the world. |
| void **repaint**() | Repaint the world. |
| void **setActOrder**(Class... classes) | Set the act order of objects in the world. |
| void **setBackground**(GreenfootImage image) | Set a background image for the world. |
| void **setBackground**(String filename) | Set a background image for the world from an image file. |
| void **setPaintOrder**(Class... classes) | Set the paint order of objects in the world. |
| void **started**() | Called by the Greenfoot system when execution has started. |
| void **stopped**() | Called by the Greenfoot system when execution has stopped. |

## Class Actor

| | |
|---|---|
| `Actor()` | Construct an Actor. |
| `void act()` | The act method is called by the Greenfoot framework to give objects a chance to perform some action. |
| `protected void addedToWorld(World world)` | This method is called by the Greenfoot system when the object has been inserted into the world. |
| `GreenfootImage getImage()` | Return the image used to represent this Actor. |
| `protected List getIntersectingObjects(Class cls)` | Return all the objects that intersect this object. |
| `protected List getNeighbours(int distance, boolean diagonal, Class cls)` | Return the neighbours to this object within a given distance. |
| `protected List getObjectsAtOffset(int dx, int dy, Class cls)` | Return all objects that intersect the given location (relative to this object's location). |
| `protected List getObjectsInRange(int r, Class cls)` | Return all objects within range 'r' around this object. |
| `protected Actor getOneIntersectingObject (Class cls)` | Return an object that intersects this object. |
| `protected Actor getOneObjectAtOffset (int dx, int dy, Class cls)` | Return one object that is located at the specified cell (relative to this object's location). |
| `int getRotation()` | Return the current rotation of the object. |
| `World getWorld()` | Return the world that this object lives in. |
| `int getX()` | Return the x-coordinate of the object's current location. |
| `int getY()` | Return the y-coordinate of the object's current location. |
| `protected boolean intersects(Actor other)` | Check whether this object intersects another given object. |
| `void setImage(GreenfootImage image)` | Set the image for this object to the specified image. |
| `void setImage(String filename)` | Set an image for this object from an image file. |
| `void setLocation(int x, int y)` | Assign a new location for this object. |
| `void setRotation(int rotation)` | Set the rotation of the object. |

## Class Greenfoot

| | |
|---|---|
| `Greenfoot()` | Constructor. |
| `static void delay(int time)` | Delay execution by a number of time steps. The size of one time step is defined by the speed slider. |
| `static String getKey()` | Get the most recently pressed key since the last time this method was called. |
| `static MouseInfo getMouseInfo()` | Return a mouse info object with information about the state of the mouse. |
| `static int getRandomNumber(int limit)` | Return a random number between 0 (inclusive) and limit (exclusive). |
| `static boolean isKeyDown(String keyName)` | Check whether a given key is currently pressed down. |

*(continued)*

## Class Greenfoot   (continued)

| | |
|---|---|
| static boolean **mouseClicked**(Object obj) | *True* if the mouse has been clicked on the given object. |
| static boolean **mouseDragEnded**(Object obj) | *True* if a mouse drag has ended. |
| static boolean **mouseDragged**(Object obj) | *True* if the mouse has been dragged on the given object. |
| static boolean **mouseMoved**(Object obj) | *True* if the mouse has been moved on the given object. |
| static boolean **mousePressed**(Object obj) | *True* if the mouse has been pressed on the given object. |
| static void **playSound**(String soundFile) | Play sound from a file. |
| static void **setSpeed**(int speed) | Set the speed of the simulation execution. |
| static void **start**() | Run (or resume) the simulation. |
| static void **stop**() | Stop the simulation. |

## Class MouseInfo

| | |
|---|---|
| Actor **getActor**() | Return the actor (if any) that the current mouse behaviour is related to. |
| int **getButton**() | The number of the pressed or clicked button (if any). |
| int **getClickCount**() | The number of mouse clicks of this mouse event. |
| int **getX**() | The current x position of the mouse cursor. |
| int **getY**() | The current y position of the mouse cursor. |
| String **toString**() | Return a string representation of this mouse event info. |

## Class GreenfootImage

| | |
|---|---|
| **GreenfootImage**(GreenfootImage image) | Create a GreenfootImage from another GreenfootImage. |
| **GreenfootImage**(int width, int height) | Create an empty (transparent) image with the specified size. |
| **GreenfootImage**(String filename) | Create an image from an image file. |
| void **clear**() | Clear the image. |
| void **drawImage**(GreenfootImage image, int x, int y) | Draw the given image onto this image. |
| void **drawLine**(int x1, int y1, int x2, int y2) | Draw a line, using the current drawing color, between the points (x1, y1) and (x2, y2). |
| void **drawOval**(int x, int y, int width, int height) | Draw an oval bounded by the specified rectangle with the current drawing color. |
| void **drawPolygon**(int[] xPoints, int[] yPoints, int nPoints) | Draw a closed polygon defined by arrays of x and y coordinates. |
| void **drawRect**(int x, int y, int width, int height) | Draw the outline of the specified rectangle. |
| void **drawstring**(String string, int x, int y) | Draw the text given by the specified string, using the current font and color. |

*(continued)*

## Class GreenfootImage  (continued)

| | |
|---|---|
| void **fill**() | Fill the entire image with the current drawing color. |
| void **fillOval**(int x, int y, int width, int height) | Fill an oval bounded by the specified rectangle with the current drawing color. |
| void **fillPolygon**(int[] xPoints, int[] yPoints, int nPoints) | Fill a closed polygon defined by arrays of x and y coordinates. |
| void **fillRect**(int x, int y, int width, int height) | Fill the specified rectangle. |
| BufferedImage **getAwtImage**() | Return the BufferedImage that backs this GreenfootImage. |
| Color **getColor**() | Return the current drawing color. |
| Color **getColorAt**(int x, int y) | Return the color at the given pixel. |
| Font **getFont**() | Get the current font. |
| int **getHeight**() | Return the height of the image. |
| int **getTransparency**() | Return the transparency of the image (range 0–255). |
| int **getWidth**() | Return the width of the image. |
| void **mirrorHorizontally**() | Mirror the image horizontally (flip around the x-axis). |
| void **mirrorVertically**() | Mirror the image vertically (flip around the y-axis). |
| void **rotate**(int degrees) | Rotate this image around the center. |
| void **scale**(int width, int height) | Scale this image to a new size. |
| void **setColor**(Color color) | Set the current drawing color. |
| void **setColorAt**(int x, int y, Color color) | Set the color at the given pixel to the given color. |
| void **setFont**(Font f) | Set the current font. |
| void **setTransparency**(int t) | Set the transparency of the image (range 0–255). |
| String **toString**() | Return a string representation of this image. |

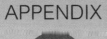

# Collision detection

In this book, various collision detection methods are used in different situations. Following is a summary of the collision detection methods available for Greenfoot actors, and a short explanation of their purpose and when to use them.

## C.1 Method summary

Greenfoot's collision detection methods can be found in the `Actor` class. There are six relevant methods. They are as follows:

`List getIntersectingObjects(Class cls)`
  *Return all the objects that intersect this object.*

`Actor getOneIntersectingObject(Class cls)`
  *Return an object that intersects this object.*

`List getObjectsAtOffset(int dx, int dy, Class cls)`
  *Return all objects that intersect the given location (relative to this object's location).*

`Actor getOneObjectAtOffset(int dx, int dy, Class cls)`
  *Return one object that is located at the specified cell (relative to this objects location).*

`List getNeighbours(int distance, boolean diagonal, Class cls)`
  *Return the neighbours to this object within a given distance.*

`List getObjectsInRange(int r, Class cls)`
  *Return all objects within range 'r' around this object.*

## C.2 Convenience methods

Two of the methods, `getIntersectingObjects` and `getObjectsAtOffset`, have associated convenience methods, starting with `getOne....`

These convenience methods work in very similar ways as the method they are based on, but they return a single actor instead of a list of actors. In cases where multiple other actors could be found (e.g., several other actors intersect with ours at the same time), the variant returning a list returns all the relevant actors. The variant returning a single actor randomly picks one of the intersecting actors and returns that one.

The purpose of these convenience methods is just to simplify code: Often, we are only interested in a single intersecting actor. In those cases, the convenience method allows us to handle the actor without having to use a list.

## C.3 Low versus high resolution

As we have seen throughout this book, the resolution (cell size) of Greenfoot worlds can vary. This is relevant for collision detection, as we will often use different methods, depending on the resolution.

We distinguish two cases: low-resolution worlds, where the entire actor image is completely contained within a single cell (Figure C.1 a) and high-resolution worlds, where the image of an actor spans multiple cells (Figure C.1 b).

**Figure C.1**

Examples of low and high resolution in Greenfoot worlds

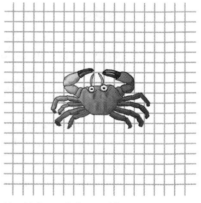

a) a low-resolution world       b) a high-resolution world

## C.4 Intersecting objects

Methods:

```
List getIntersectingObjects(Class cls)
    Return all the objects that intersect this object.

Actor getOneIntersectingObject(Class cls)
    Return an object that intersects this object.
```

These methods return other actors whose image intersects with the calling actor's image. Images intersect when any part of one image touches any part of another image. These methods are most useful in high-resolution scenarios.

Intersection is computed using bounding boxes, so overlap of fully transparent parts of the images is also treated as intersection (Figure C.2).

**Figure C.2**
Intersection of actors
using their bounding
boxes

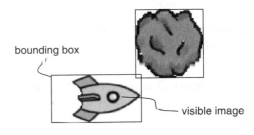

bounding box

visible image

These methods are often used to check whether one actor has run into another kind of actor. The inaccuracy resulting from using bounding boxes (rather than the visible part of the image) can often be neglected.

The parameter can be used as a filter. If a class is specified as a parameter to these methods, only objects of that class are considered and all other objects are ignored. If null is used as a parameter, any intersecting object is returned.

## C.5  Objects at offset

Methods:

`List getObjectsAtOffset(int dx, int dy, Class cls)`
   *Return all objects that intersect the given location (relative to this object's location).*

`Actor getOneObjectAtOffset(int dx, int dy, Class cls)`
   *Return one object that is located at the specified cell (relative to this objects location).*

These methods can be used to check for objects at a given offset from an actor's own current location. They are useful for both low- and high-resolution scenarios.

The *dx* and *dy* parameters specify the offset in number of cells. Figure C.3 illustrates the location at offset (2,0) from the wombat (2 cells offset along the *x* coordinate and 0 cells offset along the *y* coordinate).

**Figure C.3**
Checking a given
offset from a location
(example here:
offset 2,0)

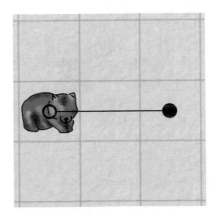

Another actor is considered to be at that offset if any part of that actor's image intersects with the center point of the specified cell. The cls parameter again provides the option to filter the objects to be considered (see above).

These methods are often used to check an area in front of an actor (to test whether it can move forward) or below an actor (to check whether it is standing on something).

## C.6 Neighbors

Method:

```
List getNeighbours(int distance, boolean diagonal, Class cls)
```
*Return the neighbours to this object within a given distance.*

This method is used to retrieve objects from cells surrounding the current actor. It is useful mainly in low-resolution scenarios.

Note the spelling of the method name: It really is getNeighbours (with British spelling)—Greenfoot is not an American system.

The parameters specify the distance from the calling actor that should be considered and whether or not diagonally positioned cells should be included. Figure C.4 illustrates the neighboring cells at distance 1, with and without diagonals included.

A distance of $N$ is defined as all cells that can be reached in $N$ steps from the actor's own position. The diagonal parameter determines whether diagonal steps are allowed in this algorithm.

As with the previous methods, the cls parameter provides the option to consider only objects of a given class.

**Figure C.4**
Example of the getNeighbours method

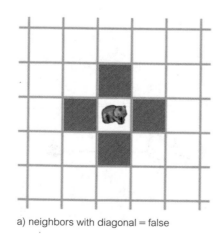
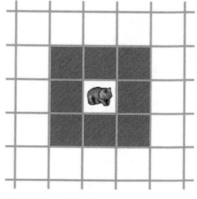

a) neighbors with diagonal = false          b) neighbors with diagonal = true

## C.7 Objects in range

Method:

```
List getObjectsInRange(int r, Class cls)
```
   *Return all objects within range 'r' around this object.*

This method returns all objects within a given range of the calling actor. An object is in range if its location is a cell whose center point is at distance r or less from the calling actor (Figure C.5). The range r is measured in cells.

**Figure C.5**
The cells in a given
range around
a location

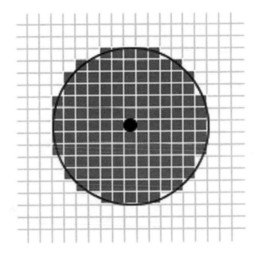

This method is mostly useful for high-resolution scenarios. As with the methods above, a class filter can be applied.

# Some Java details

## D.1 Java data types

Java knows two kinds of types: primitive types and object types. Primitive types are stored in variables directly, and they have value semantics (values are copied when assigned to another variable). Object types are stored by storing references to the object (not the object itself). When assigned to another variable, only the reference is copied, not the object.

### D.1.1 Primitive types

The following table lists all the primitive types of the Java language:

| Type name | Description | Example literals | | |
|-----------|-------------|---------|---|---|
| Integer numbers | | | | |
| byte | byte-sized integer (8 bit) | 24 | −2 | |
| short | short integer (16 bit) | 137 | −119 | |
| int | integer (32 bit) | 5409 | −2003 | |
| long | long integer (64 bit) | 423266353L | 55L | |
| Real numbers | | | | |
| float | single-precision floating point | 43.889F | | |
| double | double-precision floating point | 45.632.4e5 | | |
| Other types | | | | |
| char | a single character (16 bit) | 'm' | '?' | '\u00F6' |
| boolean | a boolean value (true or false) | true | false | |

Notes:

- *A number without a decimal point is generally interpreted as an* int, *but automatically converted to* byte, short, *or* long *types when assigned (if the value fits). You can declare a literal as* long *by putting an* L *after the number. (*l—*lower-case* L—*works as well but should be avoided because it can easily be mistaken for a one.)*

- *A number with a decimal point is of type* `double`. *You can specify a* `float` *literal by putting an* `F` *or* `f` *after the number.*
- *A character can be written as a single Unicode character in single quotes or as a four-digit Unicode value, preceded by* `\u`.
- *The two boolean literals are* `true` *and* `false`.

Because variables of the primitive types do not refer to objects, there are no methods associated with the primitive types. However, when used in a context requiring an object type, autoboxing might be used to convert a primitive value to a corresponding object.

The following table details minimum and maximum values available in the numerical types.

| Type | Minimum | Maximum |
|------|---------|---------|
| byte | −128 | 127 |
| short | −32768 | 32767 |
| int | −2147483648 | 2147483647 |
| long | −9223372036854775808 | 9223372036854775807 |
| | **Positive minimum** | **Positive maximum** |
| float | 1.4e−45 | 3.4028235e38 |
| double | 4.9e−324 | 1.7976931348623157e308 |

### D.1.2 Object types

All types not listed in the *Primitive types* section are object types. These include class and interface types from the standard Java library (such as `String`) and user-defined types.

A variable of an object type holds a reference (or 'pointer') to an object. Assignments and parameter passing have reference semantics (i.e., the reference is copied, not the object). After assigning a variable to another one, both variables refer to the same object. The two variables are said to be aliases for the same object.

Classes are the templates for objects, defining the fields and methods that each instance possesses.

Arrays behave like object types—they also have reference semantics.

## D.2 Java operators

### D.2.1 Arithmetic expressions

Java has a considerable number of operators available for both arithmetic and logical expressions. Table D.1 shows everything that is classified as an operator, including things such as type casting and parameter passing. Most of the operators are either binary operators (taking a left

**Table D.1**

Java operators,
highest precedence
at the top

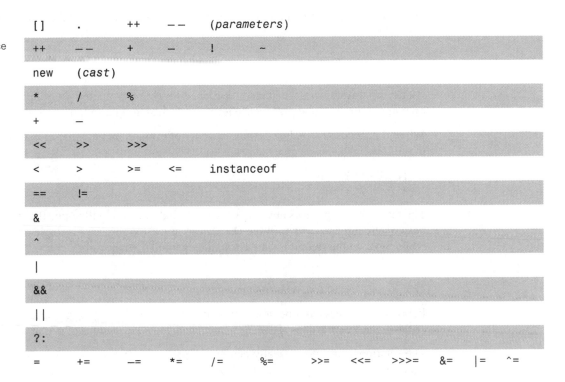

| [] | . | ++ | −− | (*parameters*) |
|----|---|----|----|----|
| ++ | −− | + | − | ! | ~ |
| new | (*cast*) |
| * | / | % |
| + | − |
| << | >> | >>> |
| < | > | >= | <= | instanceof |
| == | != |
| & |
| ^ |
| &#124; |
| && |
| &#124;&#124; |
| ?: |
| = | += | −= | *= | /= | %= | >>= | <<= | >>>= | &= | &#124;= | ^= |

and a right operand) or unary operators (taking a single operand). The main binary arithmetic operations are:

| | |
|---|---|
| + | *addition* |
| − | *subtraction* |
| * | *multiplication* |
| / | *division* |
| % | *modulus or remainder-after-division* |

The results of both division and modulus operations depend on whether their operands are integers or floating point values. Between two integer values, division yields an integer result and discards any remainder, but between floating point values a floating point value is the result:

`5 / 3` gives a result of `1`
`5.0 / 3` gives a result of `1.6666666666666667`

(Note that only one of the operands needs to be of a floating point type to produce a floating point result.)

When more than one operator appears in an expression, then *rules of precedence* have to be used to work out the order of application. In Table D.1 those operators having the highest precedence appear at the top, so we can see that multiplication, division, and modulus all take precedence over addition and subtraction, for instance. This means that both of the following examples give the result 100:

```
51 * 3 - 53
154 - 2 * 27
```

Binary operators with the same precedence level are evaluated from left to right and unary operators with the same precedence level are evaluated right to left.

When it is necessary to alter the normal order of evaluation, parentheses can be used. So both of the following examples give the result 100:

```
(205 - 5) / 2
2 * (47 + 3)
```

The main unary operators are −, !, ++, −−, [ ], and new. You will notice that ++ and −− appear in both of the top two rows in Table D.1. Those in the top row take a single operand on their left, while those in the second row take a single operand on their right.

### D.2.2 Boolean expressions

In boolean expressions, operators are used to combine operands to produce a value of either true or false. Such expressions are usually found in the test expressions of *if-else statements* and loops.

The relational operators usually combine a pair of arithmetic operands, although the tests for equality and inequality are also used with object references. Java's relational operators are:

| == | equal-to | != | not-equal-to |
|----|----------|-----|--------------|
| <  | less-than | <= | less-than-or-equal-to |
| >  | greater-than | >= | greater-than-or-equal-to |

The binary logical operators combine two boolean expressions to produce another boolean value. The operators are:

| && | and |
|----|-----|
| \|\| | or |
| ^  | exclusive-or |

In addition,

! not

takes a single boolean expression and changes it from `true` to `false`, and vice versa.

Both && and || are slightly unusual in the way they are applied. If the left operand of && is false then the value of the right operand is irrelevant and will not be evaluated. Similarly, if the left operand of || is true then the right operand is not evaluated. Thus, they are known as short-circuit operators.

## D.3  Java control structures

Control structures affect the order in which statements are executed within the body of a method or constructor. There are two main categories: *selection statements* and *loops*.

A selection statement provides a decision point at which a choice is made to follow one route through the body of a method or constructor rather than another route. An *if-else* statement involves a decision between two different sets of statements, whereas a *switch* statement allows the selection of a single option from among several.

Loops offer the option to repeat statements, either a definite or an indefinite number of times. The former is typified by the *for-each* loop and *for* loop, while the latter is typified by the *while* loop and *do* loop.

In practice, it should be borne in mind that exceptions to the above characterizations are quite common. For instance, an *if-else* statement can be used to select from among several alternative sets of statements if the *else* part contains a nested *if-else* statement; and a *for* loop can be used to loop an indefinite number of times.

## D.3.1 Selection statements

### D.3.1.1 *if-else*

The *if-else* statement has two main forms, both of which are controlled by the evaluation of a boolean expression:

```
if (expression)
{
    statements
}

if (expression)
{
    statements
}
else
{
    statements
}
```

In the first form, the value of the boolean expression is used to decide whether to execute the statements or not. In the second form, the expression is used to choose between two alternative sets of statements, only one of which will be executed.

Examples:

```
if (field.size() == 0)
{
    System.out.println("The field is empty.");
}

if (number < 0)
{
    reportError();
}
else
{
    processNumber(number);
}
```

It is very common to link *if-else* statements together by placing a second *if-else* in the *else* part of the first. This can be continued any number of times. It is a good idea to always include a final *else* part.

```
if (n < 0)
{
    handleNegative();
}
else if (number == 0)
{
    handleZero();
}
else
{
    handlePositive();
}
```

### D.3.1.2 *switch*

The *switch* statement switches on a single value to one of an arbitrary number of cases. Two possible use patterns are:

```
switch (expression)
{
    case value: statements;
        break;
    case value: statements;
        break;
    further cases omitted
    default: statements;
        break;
}

switch (expression)
{
    case value1:
    case value2:
    case value3:
        statements;
        break;
    case value4:
    case value5:
        statements;
        break;
    further cases omitted
    default:
        statements;
        break;
}
```

*Notes:*

■ *A* switch *statement can have any number of case labels.*

■ *The* break *instruction after every case is needed, otherwise the execution 'falls through' into the next label's statements. The second form above makes use of this. In this case, all three of the first values will execute the first statements section, whereas values four and five will execute the second statements section.*

- *The* `default` *case is optional. If no default is given, it may happen that no case is executed.*
- *The* `break` *instruction after the* `default` *(or the last case, if there is no* `default`*) is not needed, but is considered good style.*

Examples:

```java
switch(day)
{
    case 1: dayString = "Monday";
        break;
    case 2: dayString = "Tuesday";
        break;
    case 3: dayString = "Wednesday";
        break;
    case 4: dayString = "Thursday";
        break;
    case 5: dayString = "Friday";
        break;
    case 6: dayString = "Saturday";
        break;
    case 7: dayString = "Sunday";
        break;
    default: dayString = "invalid day";
        break;
}

switch(month)
{
    case 1:
    case 3:
    case 5:
    case 7:
    case 8:
    case 10:
    case 12:
        numberOfDays = 31;
        break;
    case 4:
    case 6:
    case 9:
    case 11:
        numberOfDays = 30;
        break;
    case 2:
        if(isLeapYear())
            numberOfDays = 29;
        else
            numberOfDays = 28;
        break;
}
```

## D.3.2 Loops

Java has three loops: *while*, *do-while*, and *for*. The *for* loop has two forms. Except for the *for-each* loop, repetition is controlled in each with a boolean expression.

### D.3.2.1 *while*

The *while* loop executes a block of statements as long as a given expression evaluates to *true*. The expression is tested before execution of the loop body, so the body may be executed zero times (i.e., not at all). This capability is an important feature of the *while* loop.

```
while (expression)
{
    statements;
}
```

Examples:

```
System.out.print("Please enter a filename: ");
input = readInput();
while (input == null)
{
    System.out.print("Please try again: ");
    input = readInput();
}

int index = 0;
boolean found = false;
while (!found && index < list.size())
{
    if(list.get(index).equals(item))
    {
        found = true;
    }
    else
    {
    index++;
    }
}
```

### D.3.2.2 *do-while*

The *do-while* loop executes a block of statements as long as a given expression evaluates to *true*. The expression is tested after execution of the loop body, so the body always executes at least once. This is an important difference from the *while* loop.

```
do
{
    statements;
} while (expression);
```

Example:

```
do
{
    System.out.print("Please enter a filename: ");
    input = readInput();
} while (input == null);
```

### D.3.2.3 *for*

The *for* loop has two different forms. The first form is also known as a *for-each* loop, and is used exclusively to iterate over elements of a collection. The loop variable is assigned the value of successive elements of the collection on each iteration of the loop.

```
for (variable-declaration : collection)
{
    statements;
}
```

Example:

```
for (String note : list)
{
    System.out.println(note);
}
```

The second form of *for* loop executes as long as a *condition* evaluates to *true*. Before the loop starts, an *initialization* statement is executed exactly once. The *condition* is evaluated before every execution of the loop body (so the loop may execute zero times). An *increment* statement is executed after each execution of the loop body.

```
for (initialization; condition; increment)
{
    statements;
}
```

Example:

```
for (int i = 0; i < text.size(); i++)
{
    System.out.println(text.get(i));
}
```

Both types of *for* loop are commonly used to execute the body of the loop a definite number of times—for instance, once for each element in a collection. A *for-each* loop cannot be used if the collection is to be modified while it is being iterated over.

# Index